Essential Bible Story Maps

39 Reference Maps and 30 Mapping Activities

Headwaters Christian Resources

© 2016 by Joe Anderson

All rights reserved
Printed in the United States of America

No part of this book may be reproduced in any form or by any electronic or mechanical means, including information storage and retrieval systems, except for brief quotations in printed reviews, without the prior permission of the author.

ISBN: 978-1-945413-94-0

Introduction

Stories happen to people, and they happen in places. As we read the biblical stories, we pay a lot of attention to the people, but we often ignore the places.

That is a mistake. The biblical authors troubled themselves to write down the places for a reason. The setting matters. In some stories, it matters because the topography is important to the story — as, for example, when David faces Goliath in the Valley of Elah.

In some stories, particular places become characters in the story. Bethel is the place Jacob had his dream of angels when he was fleeing his brother Esau. Later in his life, God called him back to Bethel to sacrifice, fulfilling the vow he had made there years before. Further into the story, Bethel becomes home of the Israelite kings, and inverts its role: sacrifices at Bethel become an abomination (Amos 4:4), and Bethel becomes a place to avoid rather than a place to seek (Amos 5:5). God will judge it (Hosea 10:4), even though it still retains its association with Jacob's faithfulness (Hosea 12:4).

The paths that are walked in the biblical story become signals of repeated themes. Long before the Exodus, Abraham had walked a similar path to Egypt and escaped by God's grace. The exile was a reversal of Abraham's journey from Ur of the Chaldees. And Jesus carried His cross to the same place that David had carried the head of Goliath.

This is not a Bible atlas. Those are good resources and you should have one on hand, but we were aiming for something different here. This is a companion to reading the Story of the Bible from beginning to end. You can either follow along with the characters on the reference maps, or mark their paths yourself on the activity maps. As biblical storytellers, we wanted to be able to show our hearers the places where the stories took place, so that they could immerse themselves that much further in the Story.

May God bless you with insight as you read and study.

Joe Anderson

Englewood, Colorado

Reference Maps

Abram's Journey to the Promised Land	8
Abraham Offers Isaac	9
Abraham's Servant Finds Isaac a Wife	10
Jacob's Journey to Haran and Back	11
Jacob in the Land of Canaan	12
Joseph Betrayed into Egypt	13
Judah and Tamar	14
Joseph's Brothers go to Egypt to buy Grain	15
The Journey from Sinai to Kadesh	16
Israel Defeats the Amorite Alliance	17
The Southern Campaign	18
The Northern Campaign	19
Boundaries of the Twelve Tribes	20
Jael and Sisera	21
Samson and the Philistines	22
The Journey of the Ark	23
The Kingdom of Israel Under Solomon	24
The Divided Kingdom	25
Israel and Judah's Exile	26
The Four Empires of Daniel's Statue	28
Mary and Joseph's Journey to Bethlehem	29
Jesus' Family Flees to Egypt	30
Jesus Amazes the Teachers in the Temple	31
Jesus' Ministry Begins: His First Trip to Judea	32
Jesus' Second Trip to Judea	33
Jesus' Popularity Grows	34
Jesus Rejected in Galilee (1)	35
Jesus Rejected in Galilee (2)	36
Jesus Rejected in Galilee (3)	37
Jesus' Final Journey to Jerusalem	38
Philip's Missionary Journey	39
Peter's Missionary Journey	40
Paul's First Missionary Journey	41
Paul's Second Missionary Journey	42
Paul's Third Missionary Journey	43
Paul's Journey to Rome	44
The Topography of Israel	45
Land Cover and Vegetation	46

Mapping Activities

Abram's Journey to the Promised Land	48
Abraham's Servant Finds Isaac a Wife	49
Jacob's Journey to Haran and Back	50
Jacob in the Land of Canaan	51
Joseph Betrayed into Egypt	52
Judah and Tamar	53
Joseph's Brothers go to Egypt to buy Grain	54
The Exodus from Egypt	55
The Journey from Sinai to Kadesh	56
Israel Defeats the Amorite Alliance	57
The Southern Campaign	58
The Northern Campaign	59
Boundaries of the Twelve Tribes	60
Jael and Sisera	61
Samson and the Philistines	62
Mary and Joseph's Journey to Bethlehem	63
Jesus' Family Flees to Egypt	64
Jesus Amazes the Teachers in the Temple	65
Jesus' Ministry Begins: His First Trip to Judea	66
Jesus' Second Trip to Judea	67
Jesus' Popularity Grows	68
Jesus Rejected in Galilee (1)	69
Jesus Rejected in Galilee (2)	70
Jesus Rejected in Galilee (3)	71
Jesus' Final Journey to Jerusalem	72
Philip's Missionary Journey	73
Peter's Missionary Journey	74
Paul's First Missionary Journey	75
Paul's Second Missionary Journey	76
Paul's Third Missionary Journey	77
Paul's Journey to Rome	78

Old Testament Reference Maps

Abram's Journey to the Promised Land

Scale: 0 — 100 — 200 mi

1. Abram traveled from Ur to Haran with his father Terah and settled there (Gen 11:31).

2. God called Abram from Haran to Canaan (Gen 12:1).

3. Abram arrived in the land, heard from the Lord at Shechem and worshipped at Bethel (Gen 12:6-8).

Regions: Mesopotamia, Shinar, Paddan-aram, Lebanon, Bashan, Moab, Negeb, Midian

Bodies of water: Great Sea, Sea of Galilee, Salt Sea, Jordan, Tigris, Euphrates

Cities and places: Ur, Eridu, Uruk, Lagash, Girsu, Umma, Adab, Nippur, Isin, Dilbat, Kish, Borsippa, Babel, Babylon, Sippar, Akkad, Erech, Der, Eshnunna, Samarra, Ashur, Nineveh, Mari, Haran, Ebla, Tarsus, Cyprus, Damascus, Sidon, Tyre, Shechem, Lod, Bethel, Jebus, Jericho, Hebron, Beersheba, Kadesh, Sodom, Gomorrah, Zoar, Amalek

Abraham's Servant Finds Isaac a Wife

2. The servant providentially met Rebekah in Paddan-aram (Gen 24:10-57).

1. Abraham sent his servant to his home country to find a wife for Isaac (Gen 24:1-10).

3. Isaac came from Beer-lahai-roi and met Rebekah (Gen 24:58-67).

Jacob's Journey to Haran and Back

1. Jacob set out in haste from Beersheba and camped at Bethel (formerly Luz) before continuing on to Paddan-aram (Gen 28:10-29:1).

2. Jacob served in Laban's house for 20 years before fleeing back to Canaan (Gen 31:1-21).

3. Laban caught up with Jacob in the hill country of Gilead. Then Jacob came to Peniel where he wrestled with God (Gen 31:22-32:31).

4. Esau came up from Seir and met Jacob in peace; Jacob then continued on as far as Shechem (Gen 33).

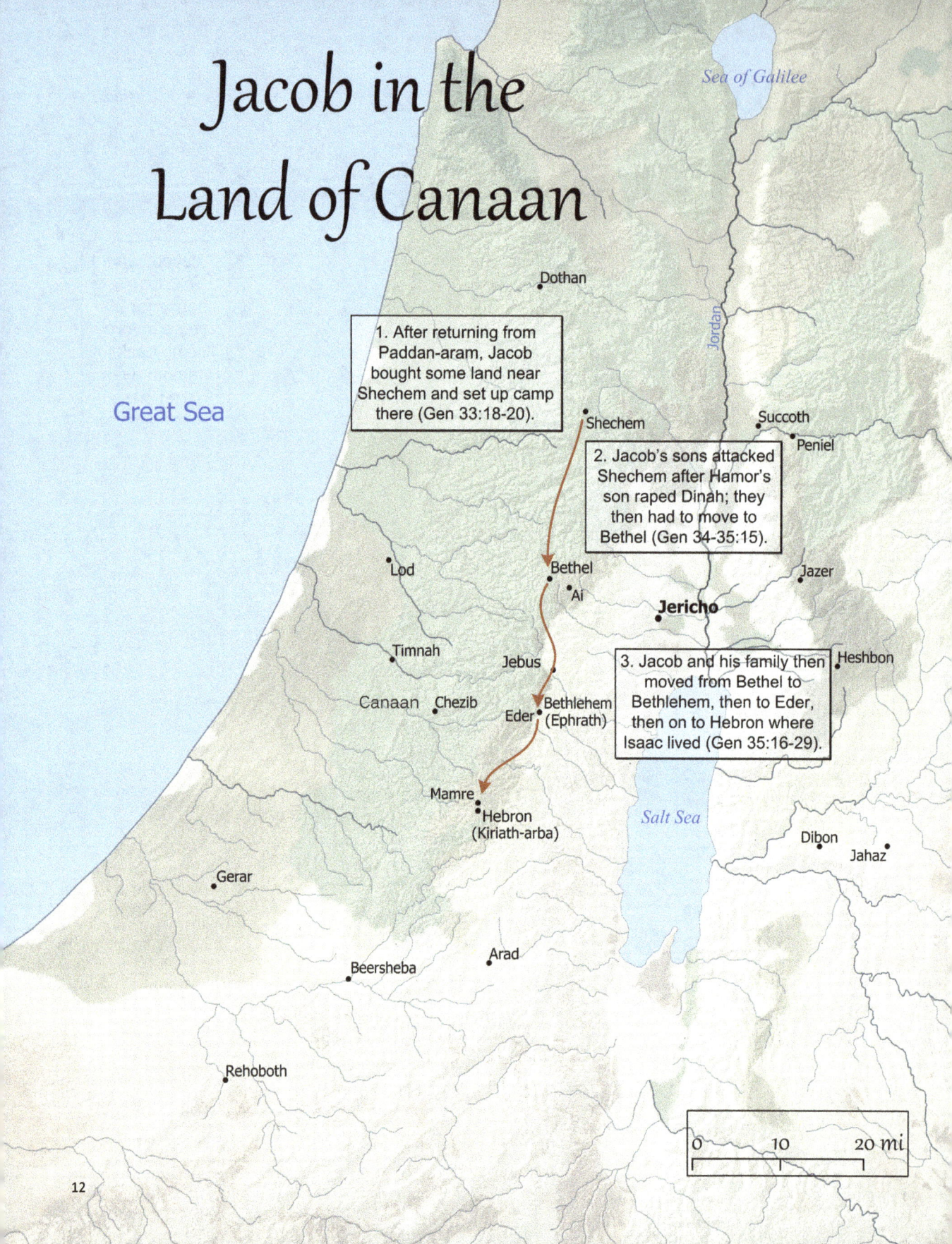

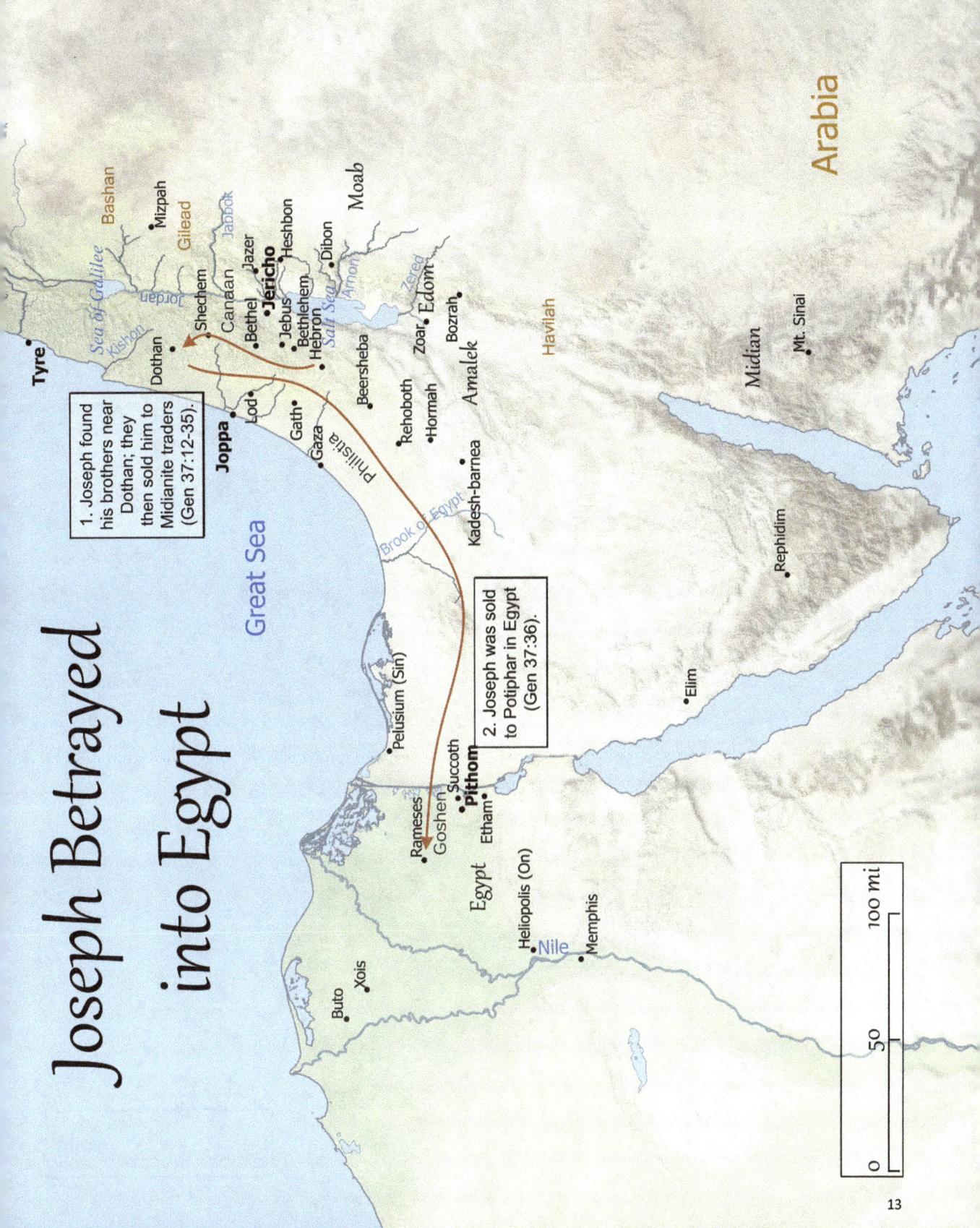

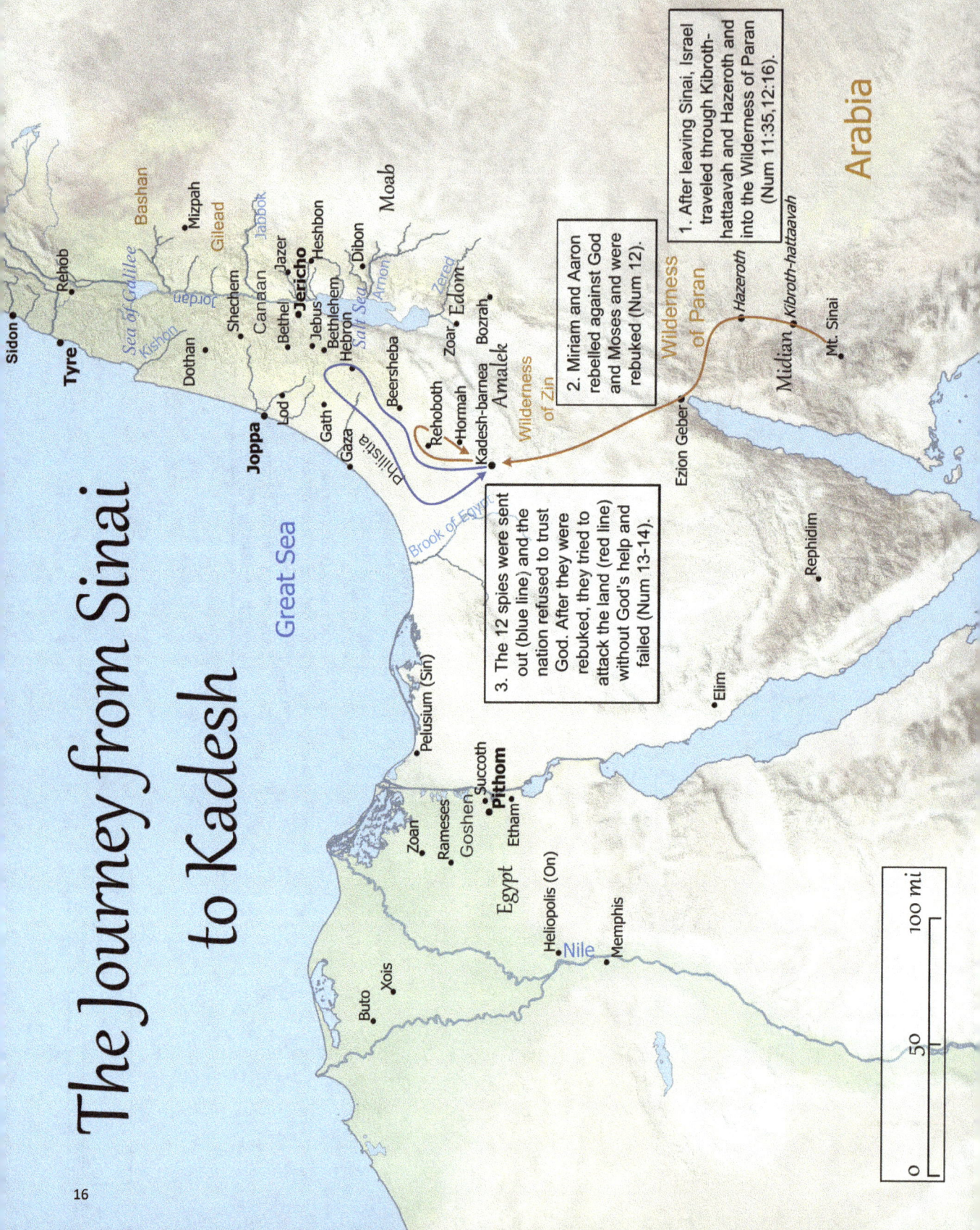

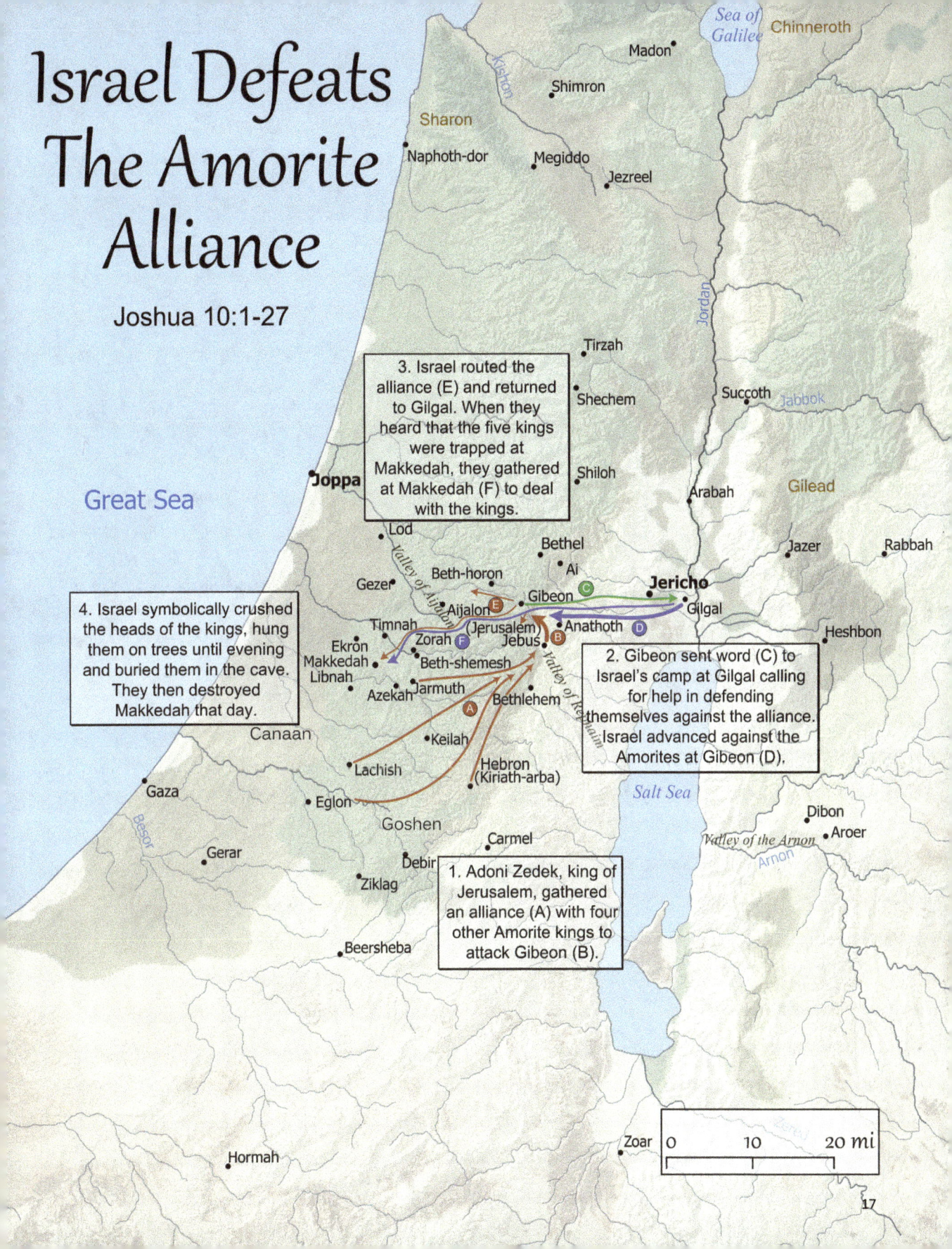

Samson and the Philistines

Judges 14

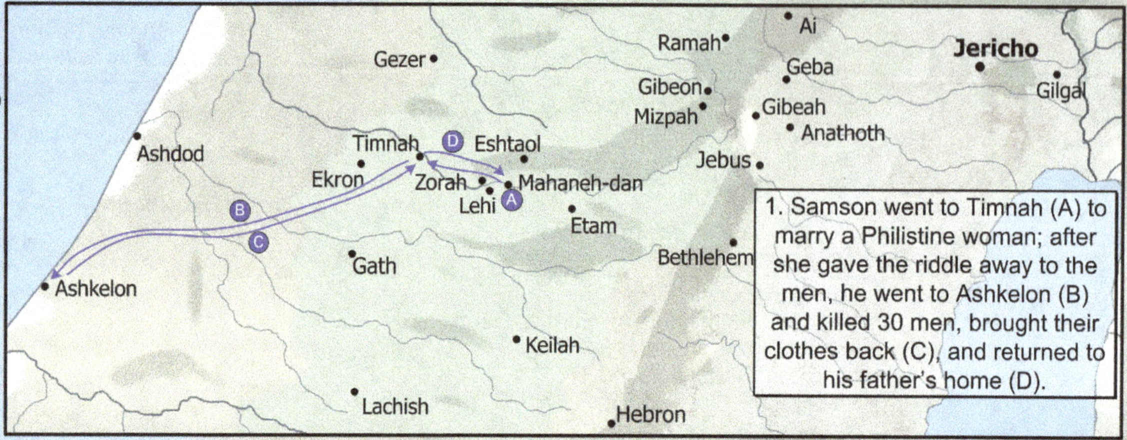

1. Samson went to Timnah (A) to marry a Philistine woman; after she gave the riddle away to the men, he went to Ashkelon (B) and killed 30 men, brought their clothes back (C), and returned to his father's home (D).

Judges 15

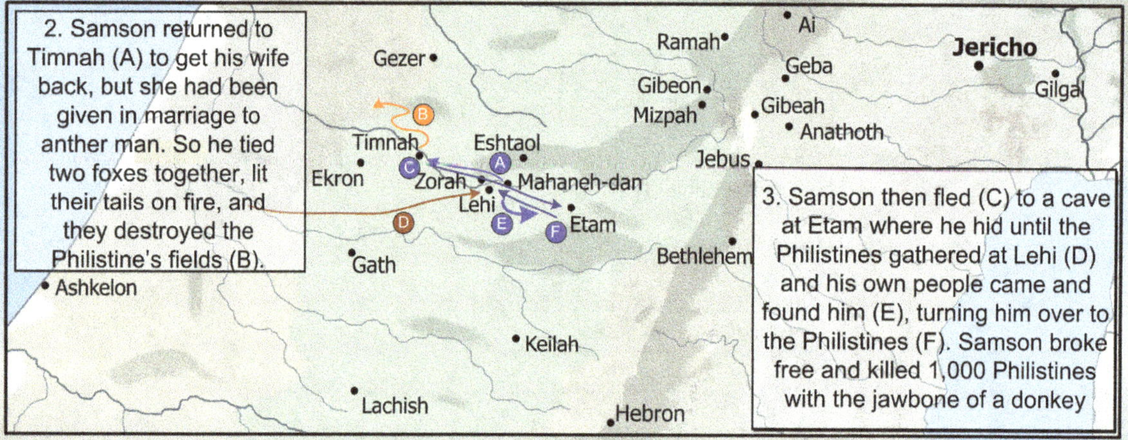

2. Samson returned to Timnah (A) to get his wife back, but she had been given in marriage to anther man. So he tied two foxes together, lit their tails on fire, and they destroyed the Philistine's fields (B).

3. Samson then fled (C) to a cave at Etam where he hid until the Philistines gathered at Lehi (D) and his own people came and found him (E), turning him over to the Philistines (F). Samson broke free and killed 1,000 Philistines with the jawbone of a donkey

Judges 16

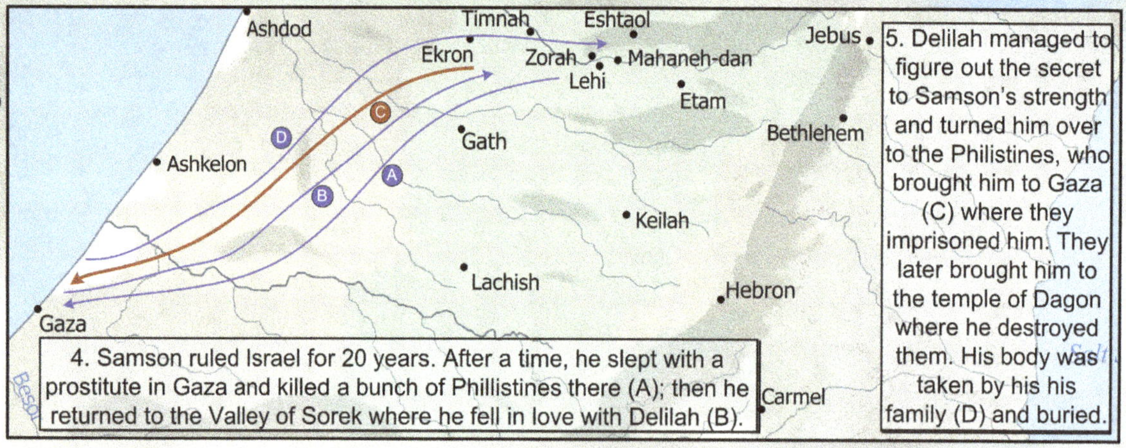

4. Samson ruled Israel for 20 years. After a time, he slept with a prostitute in Gaza and killed a bunch of Phillistines there (A); then he returned to the Valley of Sorek where he fell in love with Delilah (B).

5. Delilah managed to figure out the secret to Samson's strength and turned him over to the Philistines, who brought him to Gaza (C) where they imprisoned him. They later brought him to the temple of Dagon where he destroyed them. His body was taken by his his family (D) and buried.

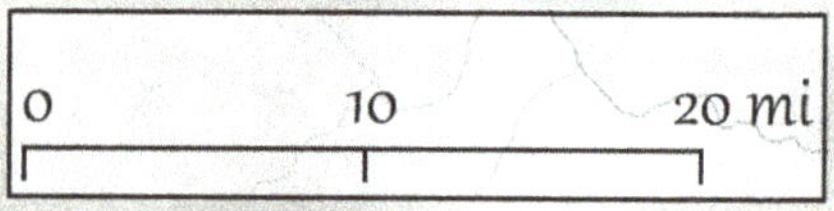

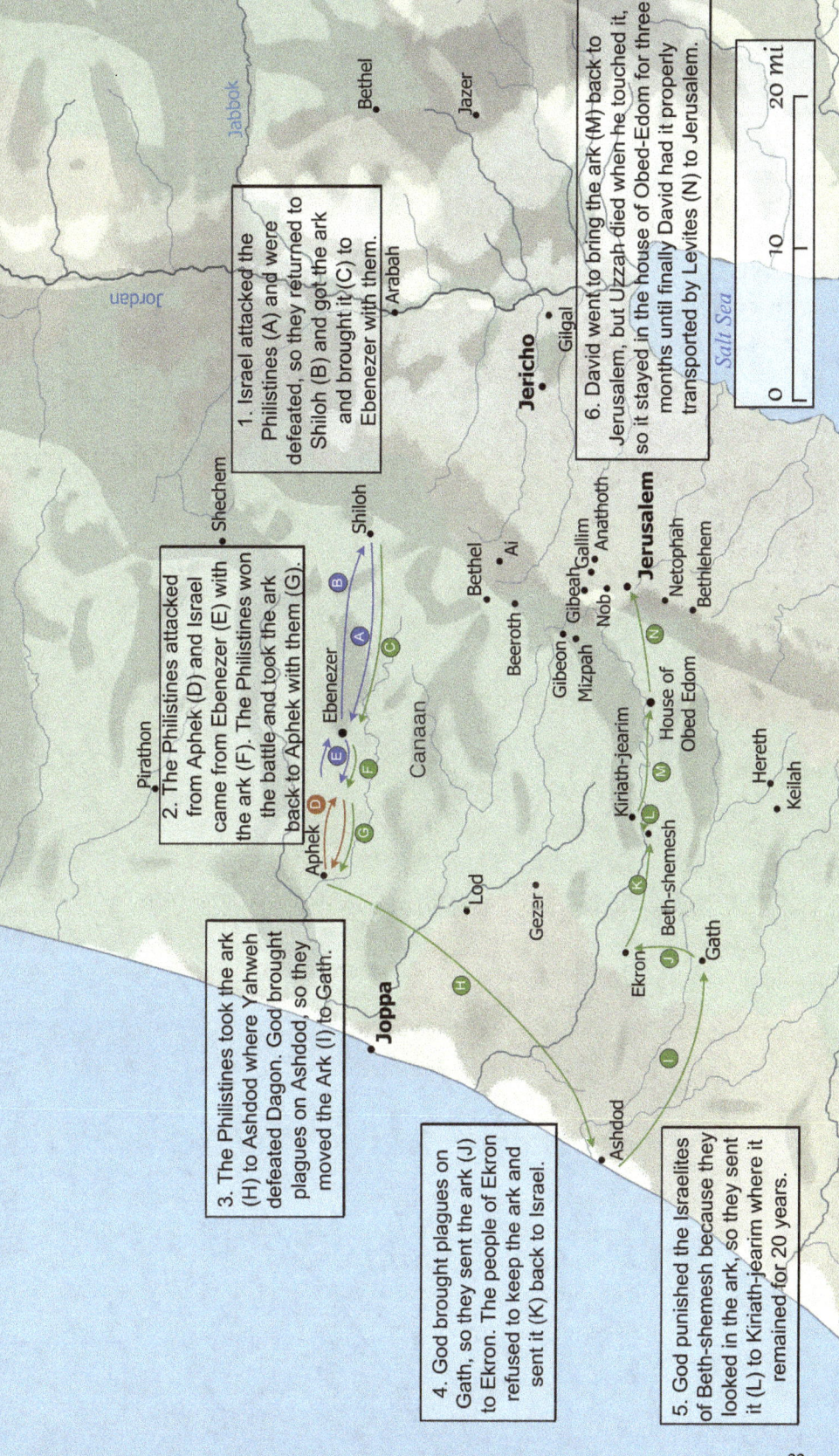

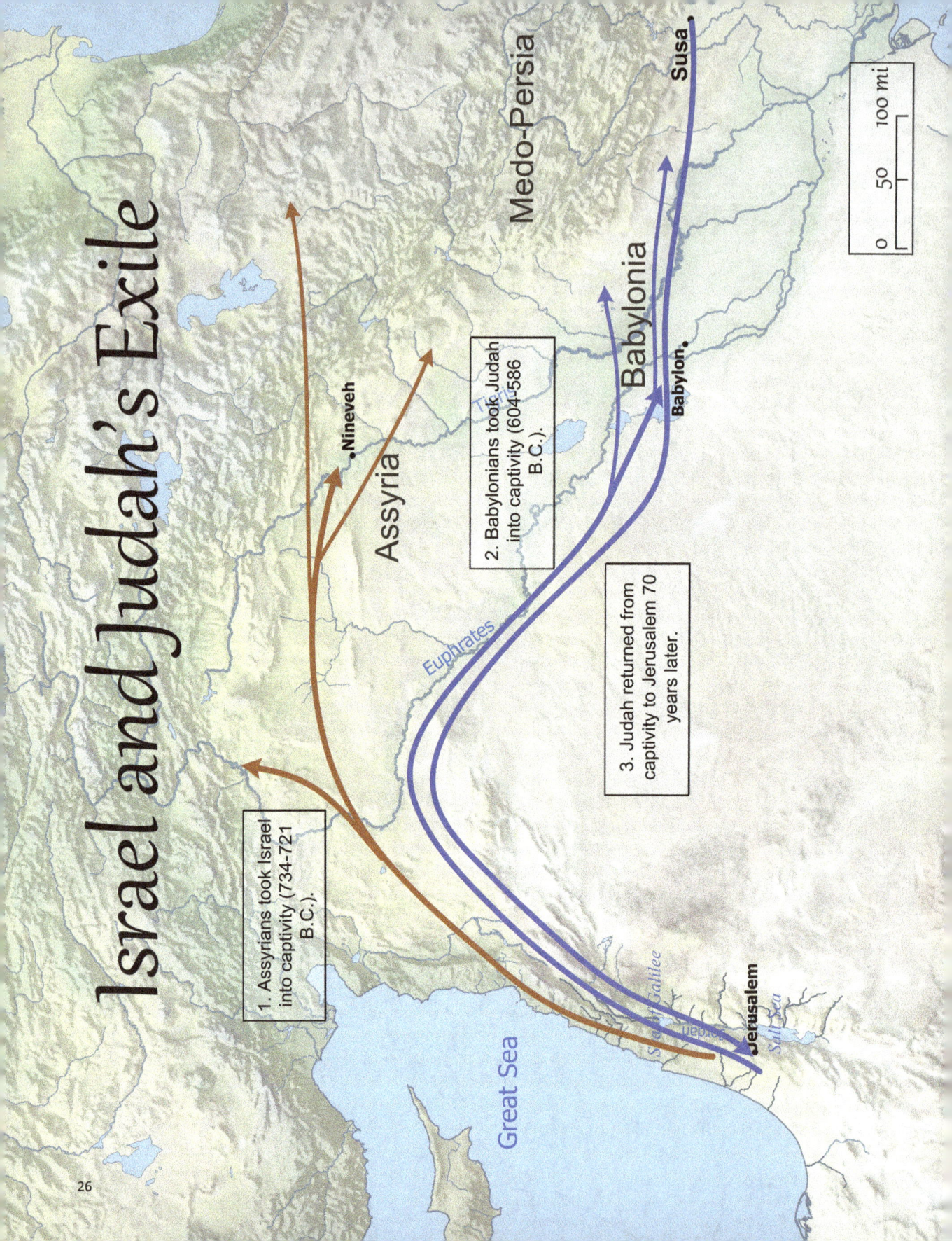

New Testament Reference Maps

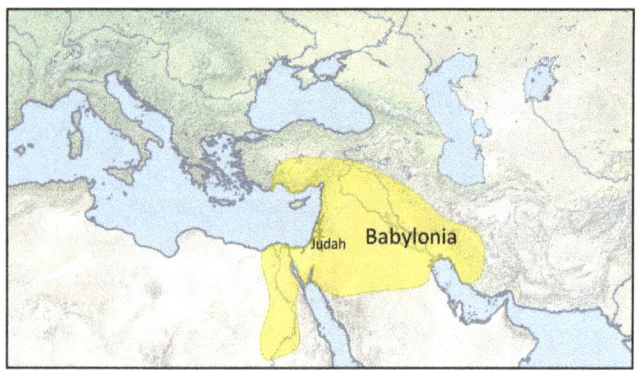

BABYLONIA (626-539 B.C.)

- Head of gold in Daniel's statue
- Destroyed Jerusalem and the temple and carried Judah into captivity in 586 B.C.

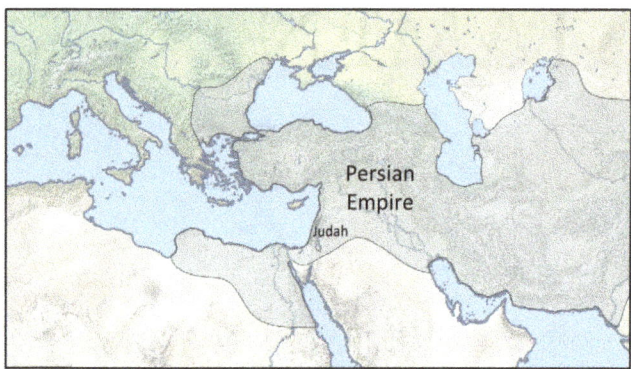

PERSIAN EMPIRE (539-332 BC)

- Chest and arms of silver in Daniel's statue
- Darius captured Babylon in 539 B.C.

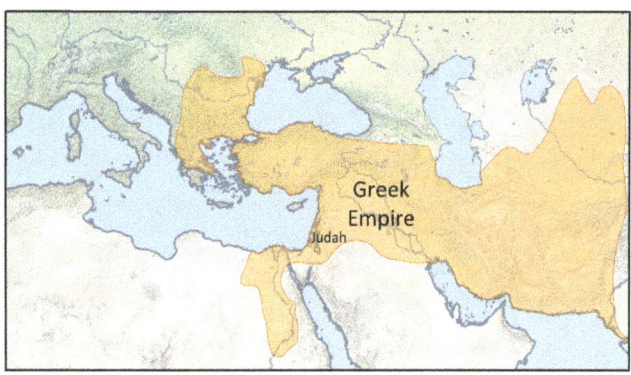

GREEK EMPIRE (332-63 BC)

- Belly and thighs of bronze in Daniel's statue
- Alexander the Great defeated the Persians in 332 B.C.

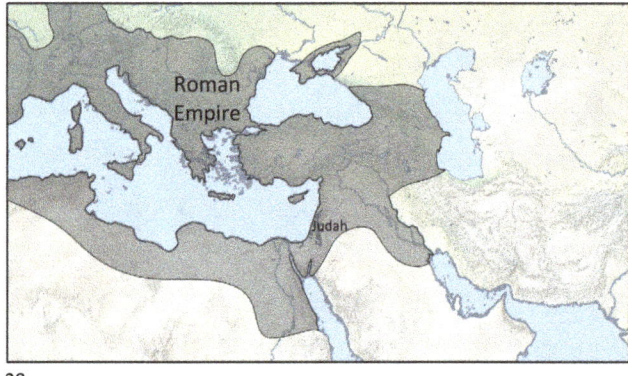

ROMAN EMPIRE (63 BC- 476 AD)

- Legs of iron and feet of iron and clay in Daniel's statue
- Roman General Pompey conquered Jerusalem in 63 B.C.

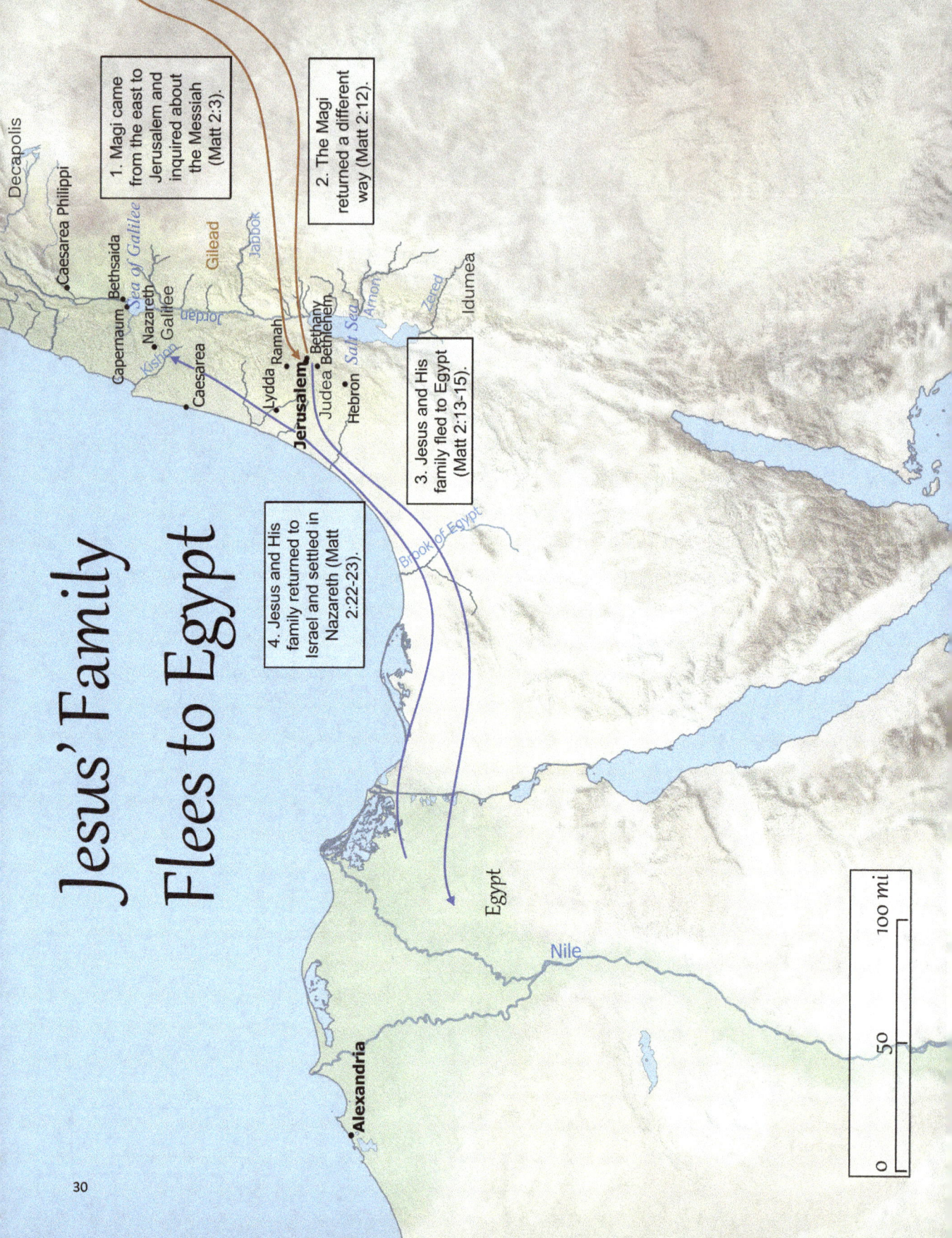

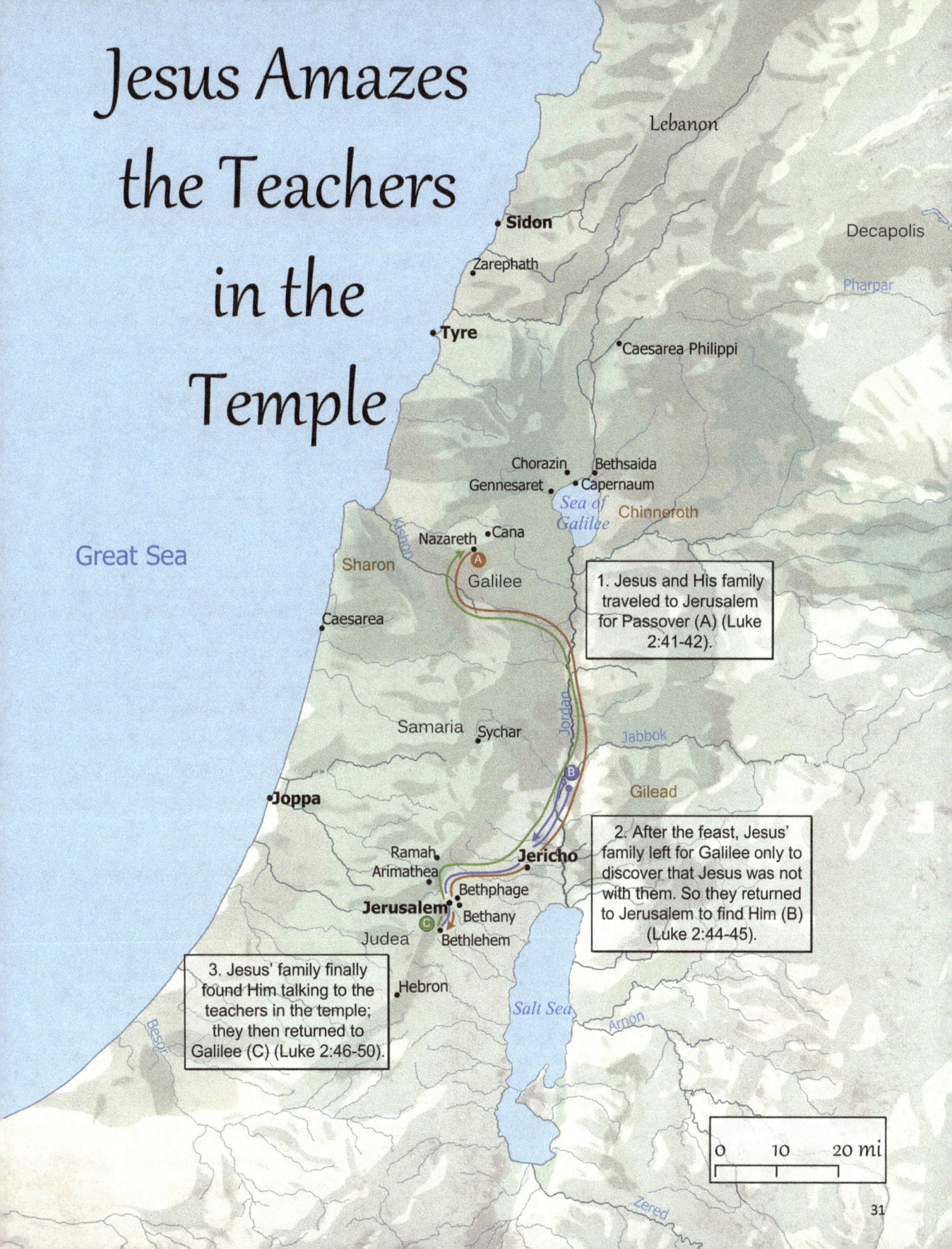

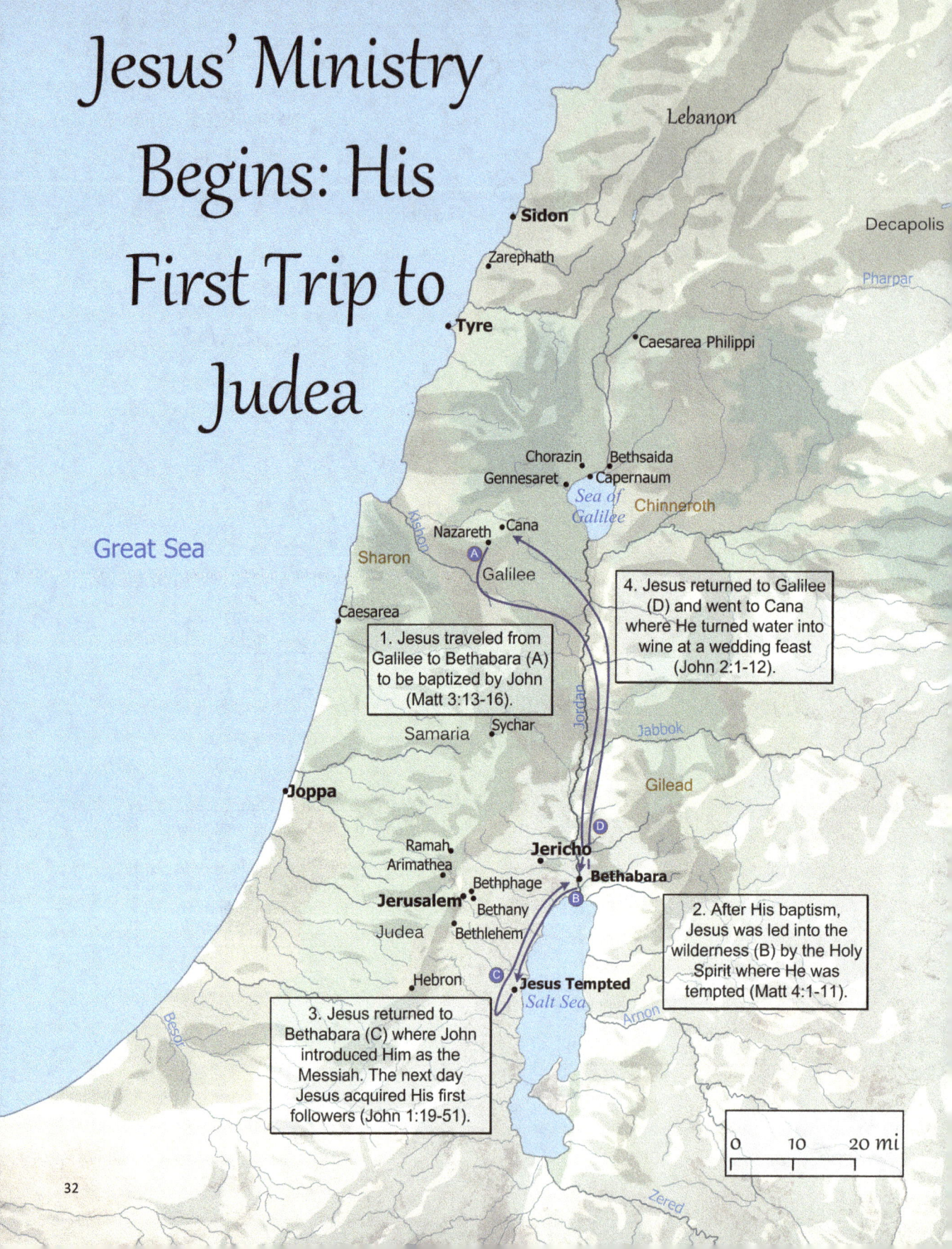

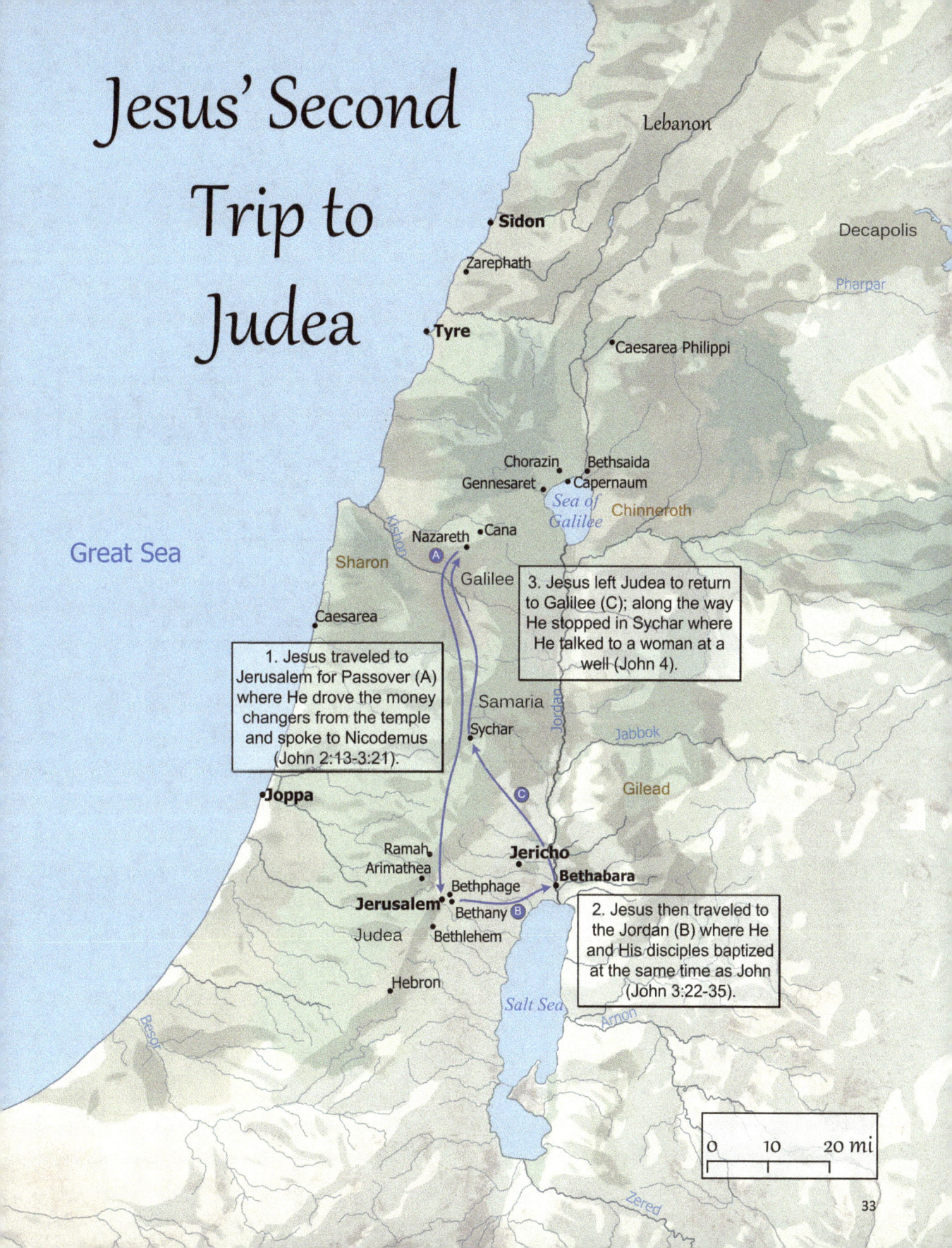

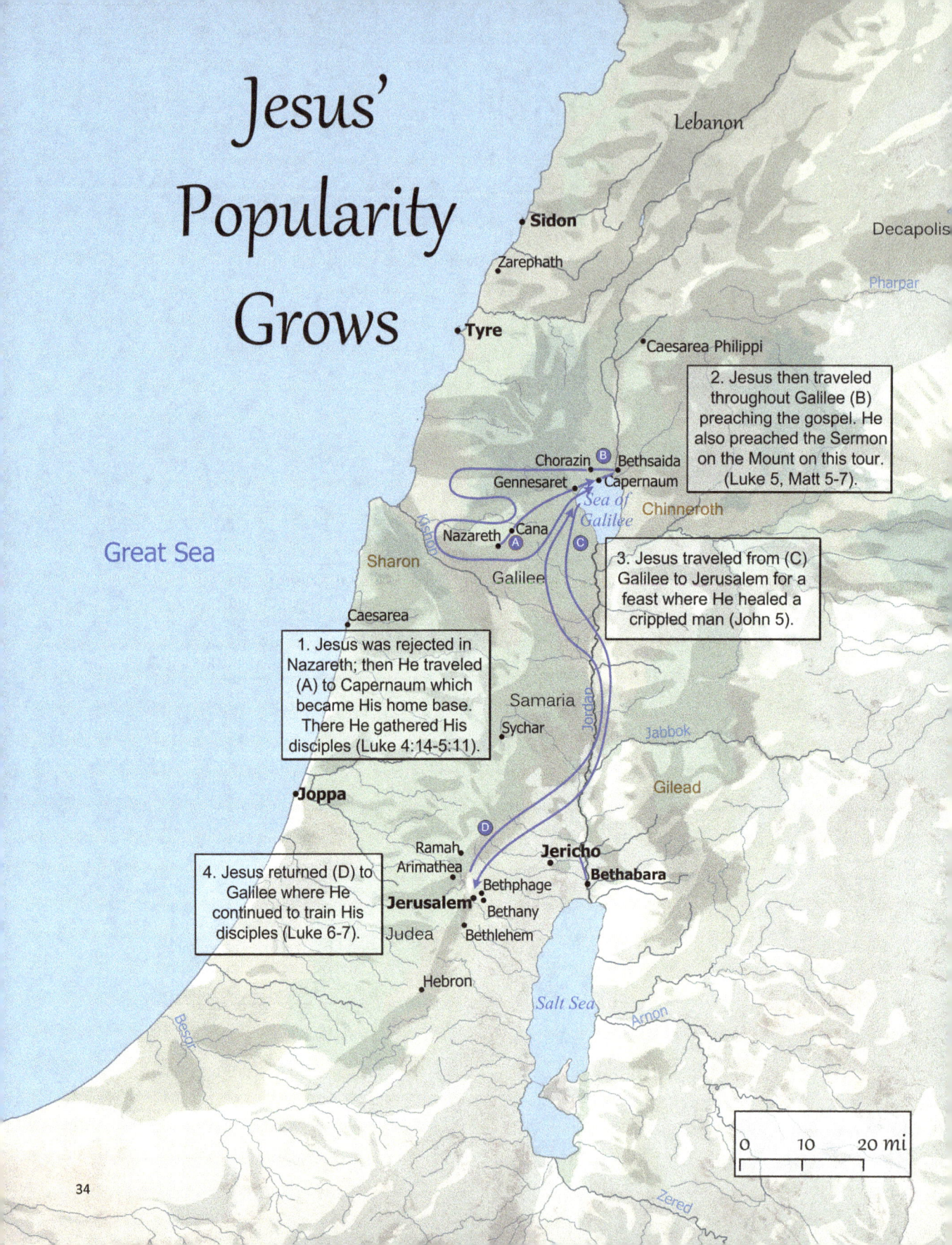

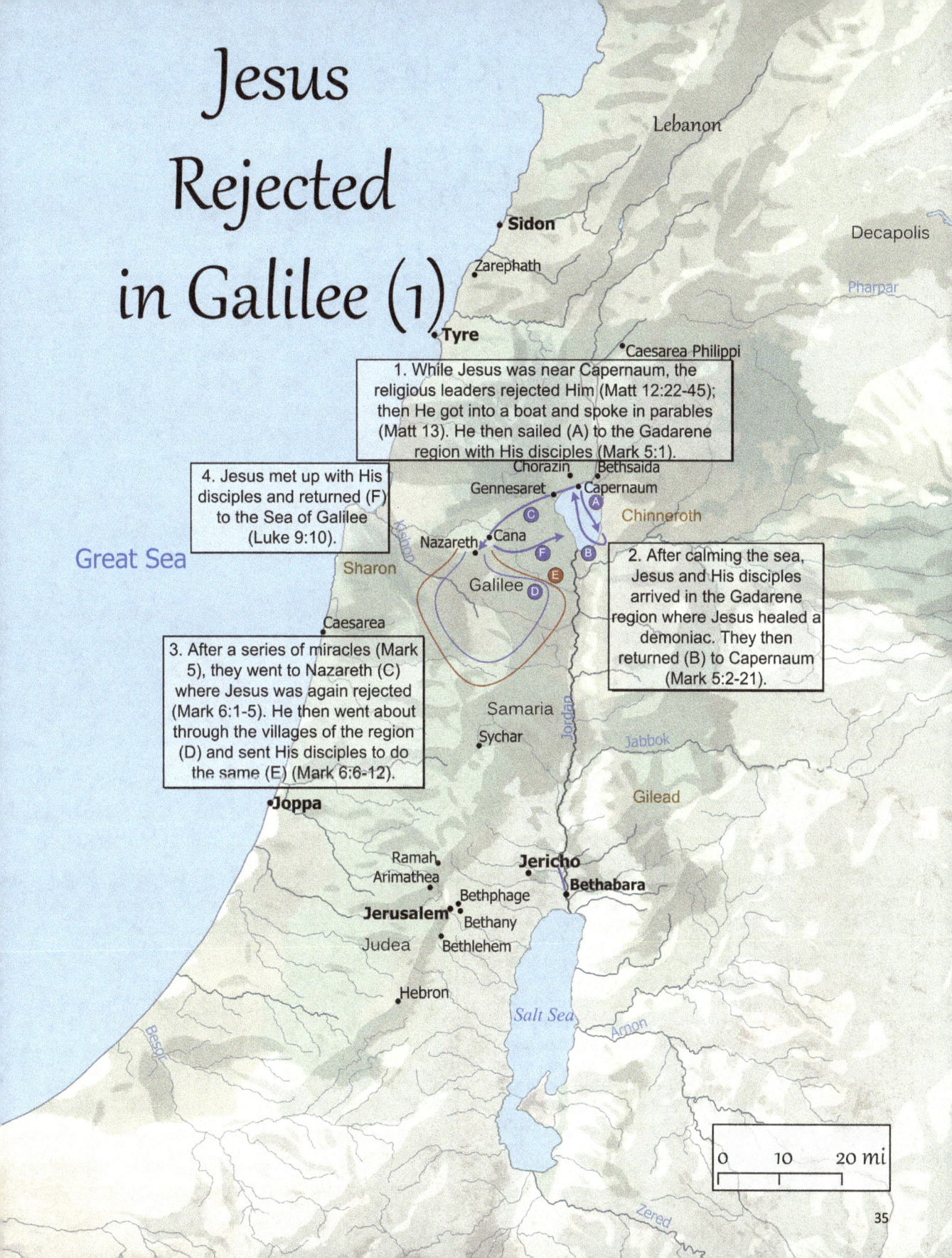

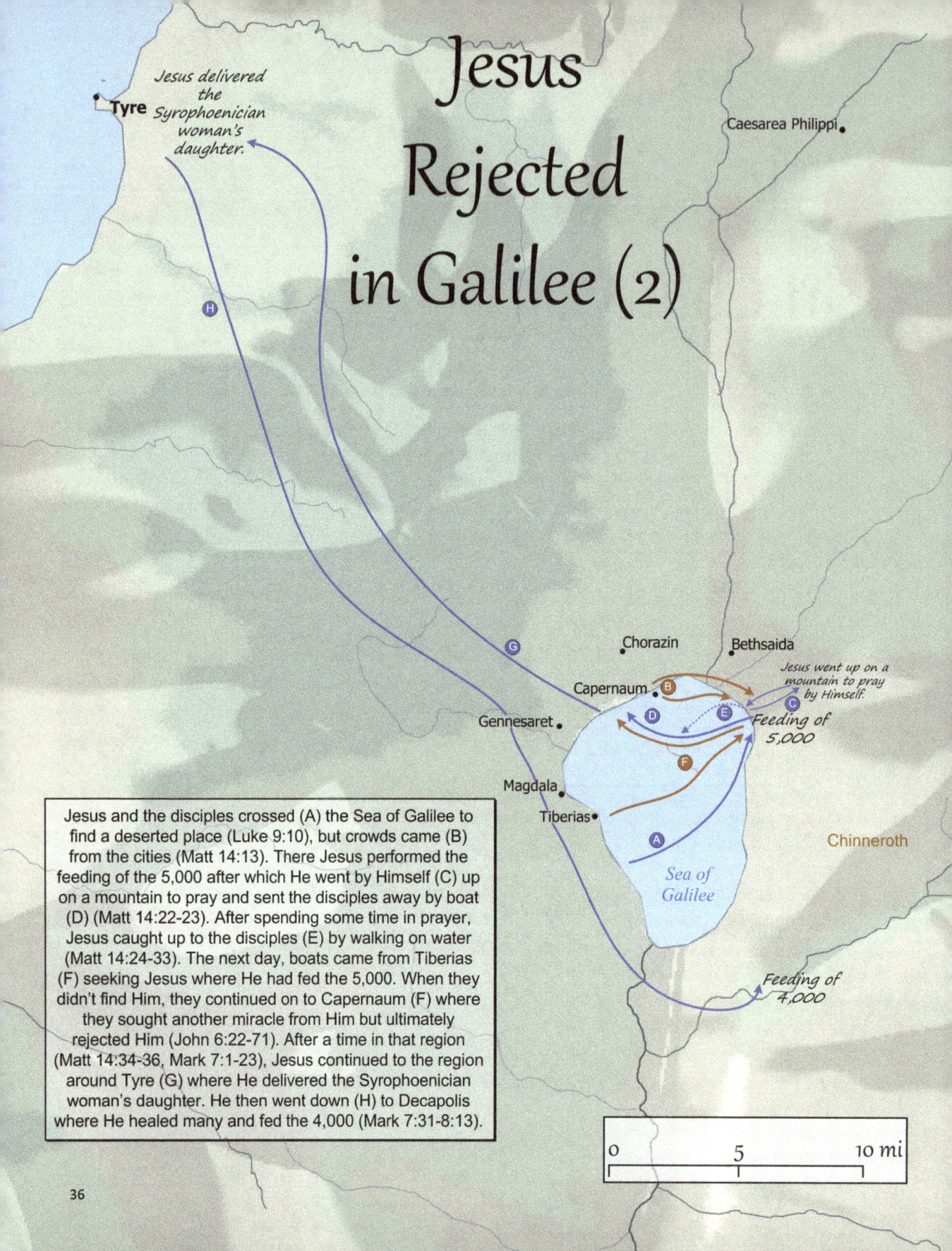

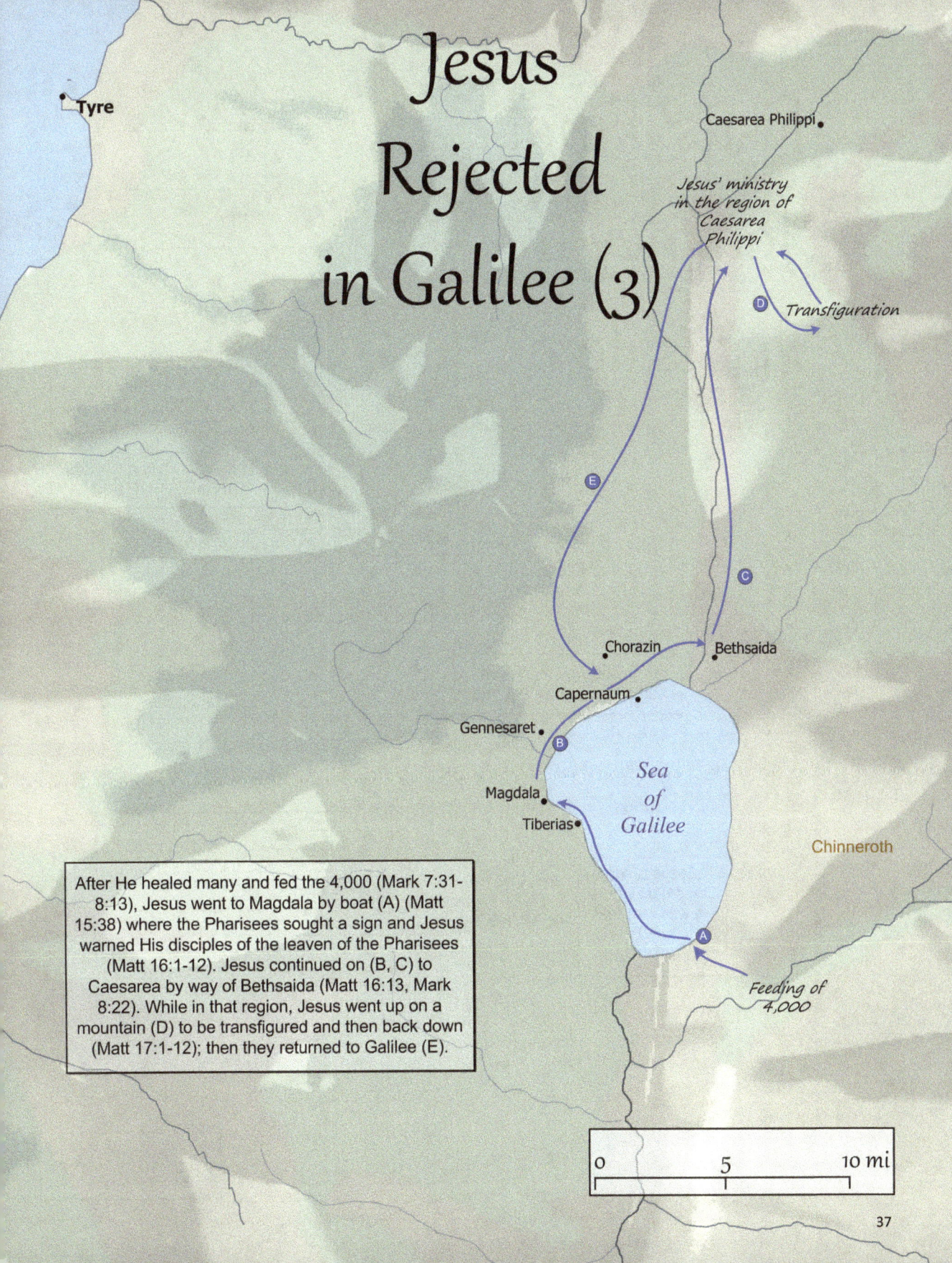

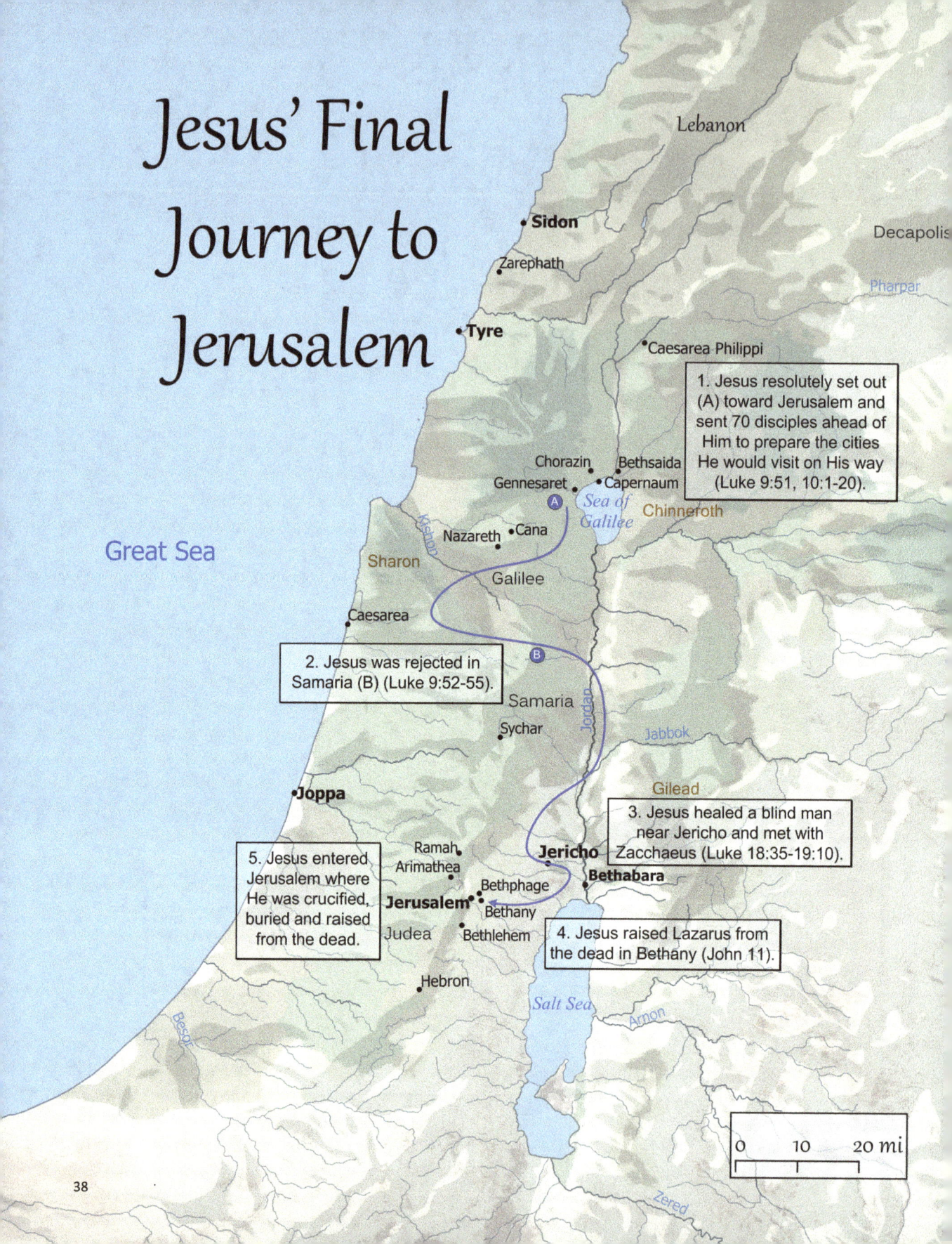

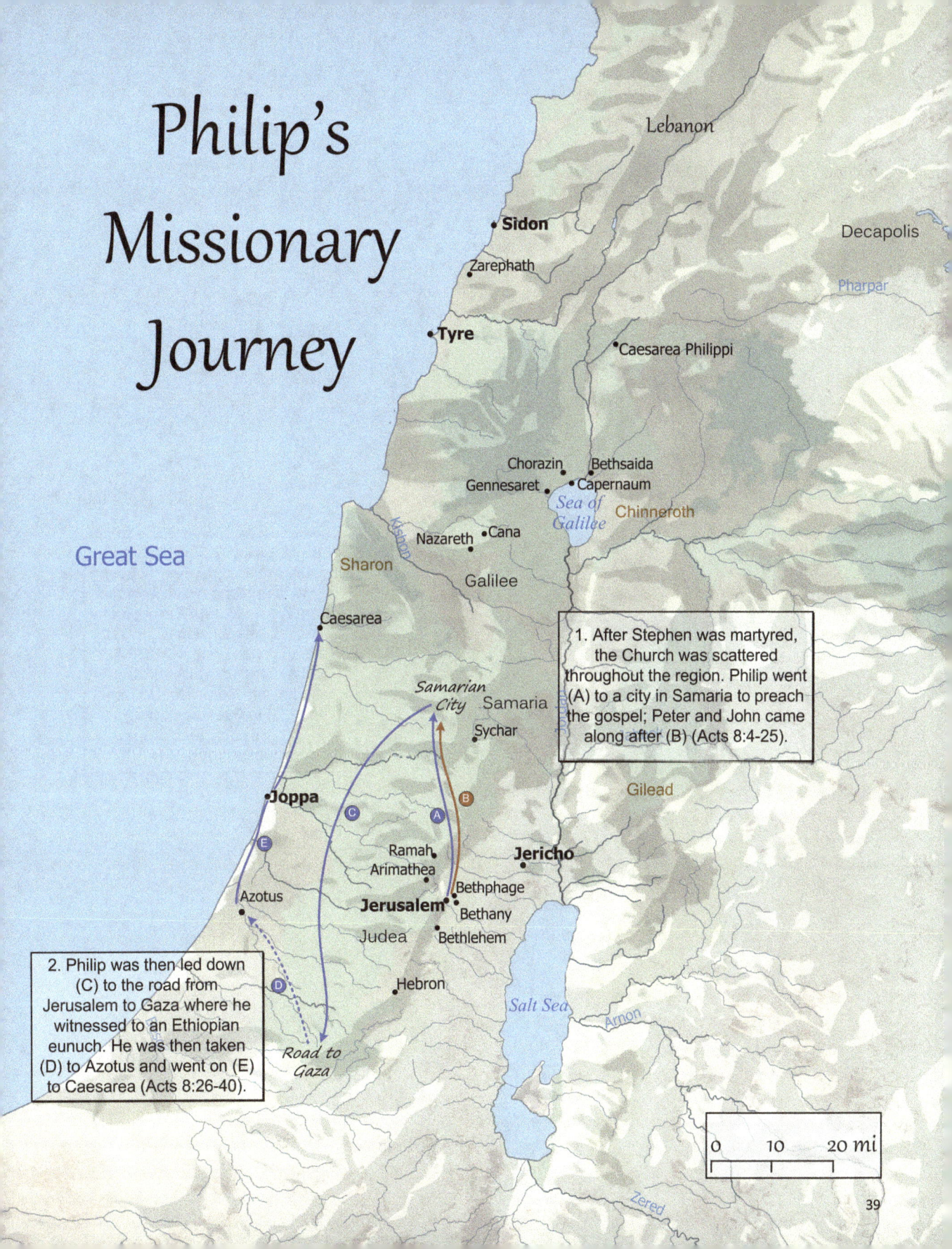

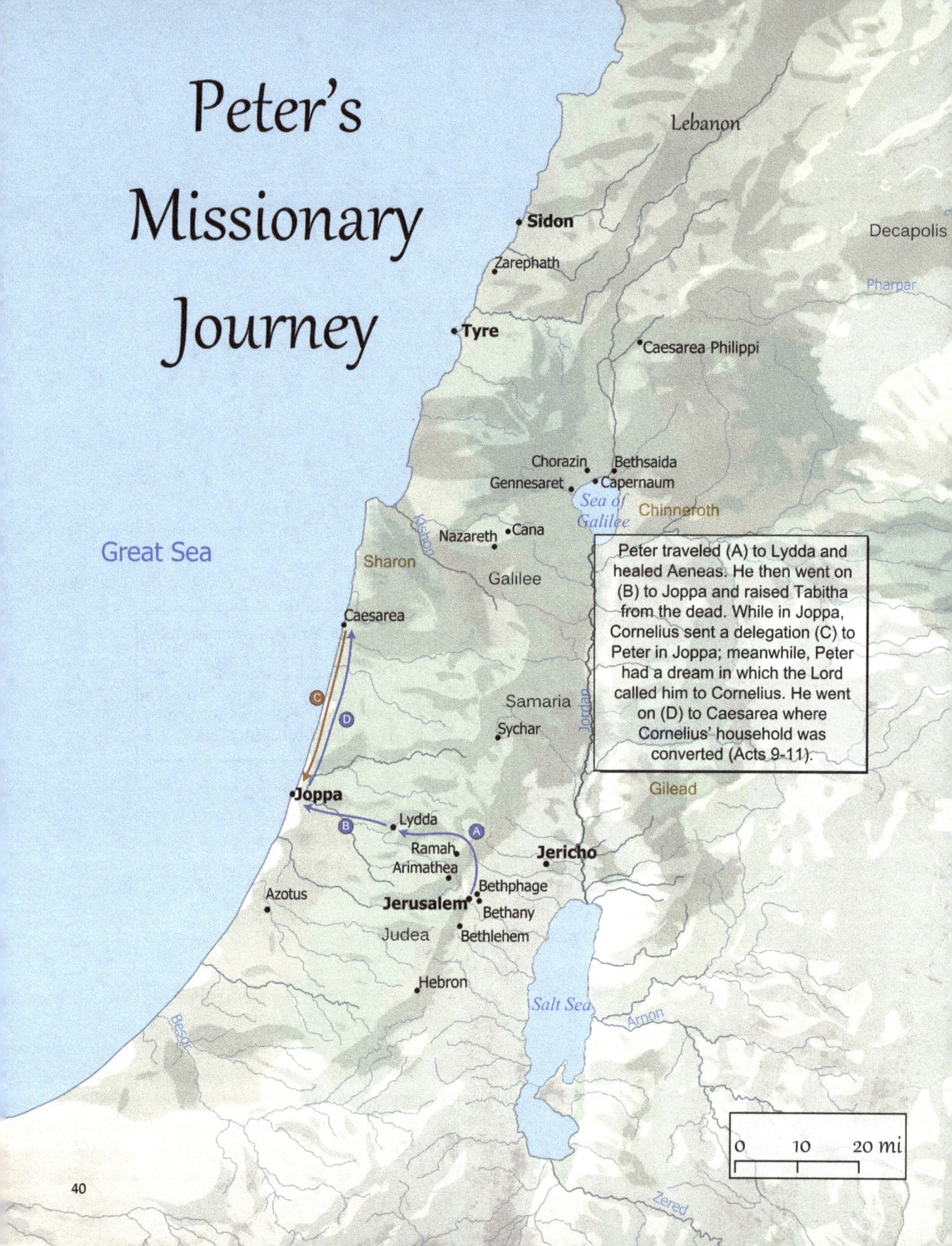

Mapping Activities

Abram's Journey to the Promised Land

Mapping Activity

Read Genesis 11:31–12:8, then mark and label Abram's journey to the promised land.

Abraham's Servant Finds Isaac a Wife

Mapping Activity

Read Genesis 24, then mark and label Abraham's servants' journey to find a wife for Isaac.

Map labels:

- Haran
- Paddan-aram
- Lebo-hamath
- Great Sea
- Lebanon
- Sidon
- Damascus
- Tyre
- Abana
- Pharpar
- Bashan
- Kishon
- Sea of Galilee
- Mizpah
- Canaan
- Shechem
- Jordan
- Succoth
- Jabbok
- Joppa
- Bethel
- Jazer
- Lod
- Jericho
- Jebus
- Heshbon
- Gath
- Bethlehem
- Gaza
- Hebron
- Dibon
- Philistia
- Salt Sea
- Arnon
- Moab
- Beersheba
- Rehoboth
- Zered
- Hormah
- Zoar
- Edom
- Beer-lahai-roi
- Bozrah
- Brook of Egypt
- Brook of the Arabah
- Amalek

0 50 100 mi

49

Jacob's Journey to Haran and Back

Mapping Activity

Read Genesis 28:10-29:14 and 31:1-33:3, then mark and label Jacob's journey to Haran and back.

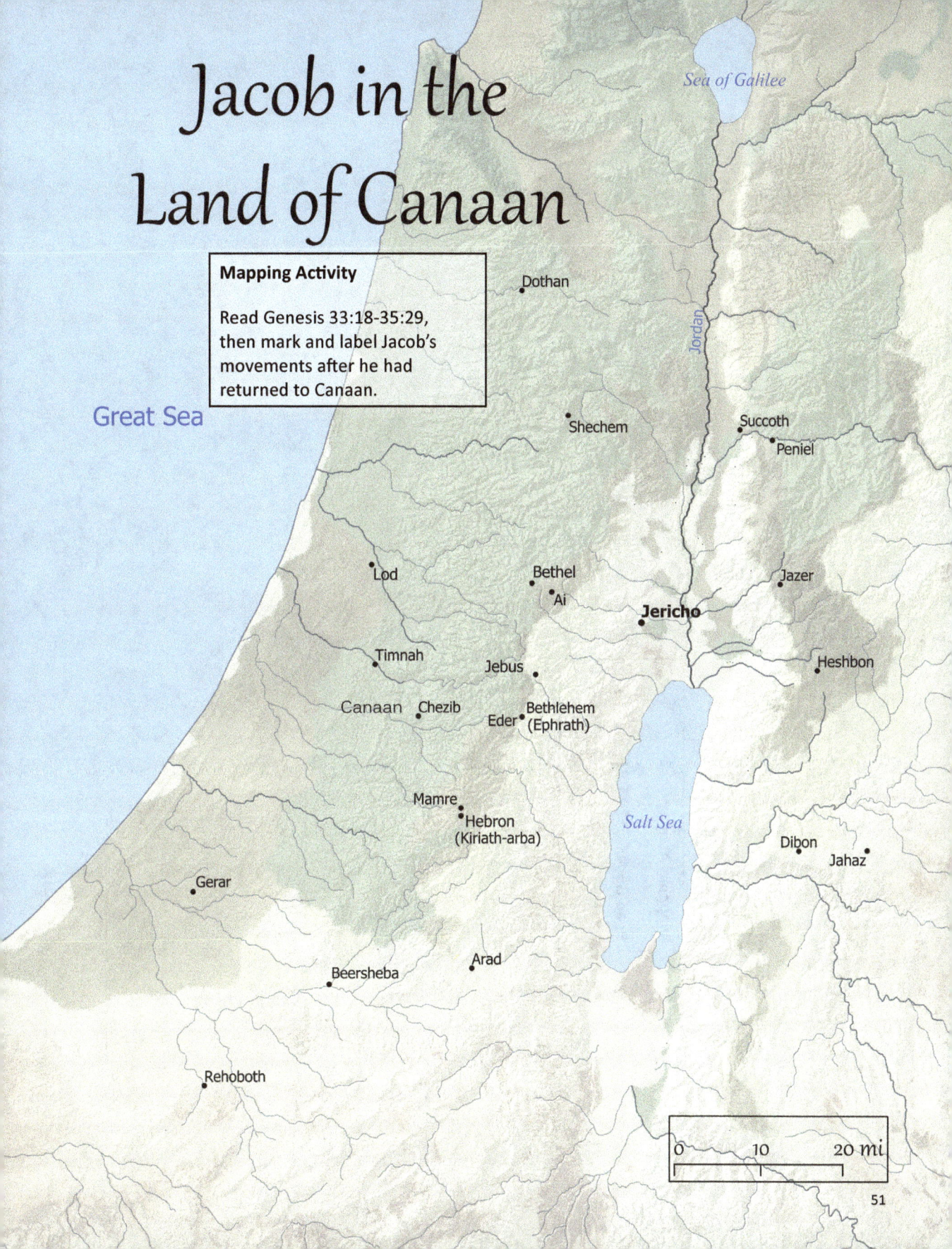

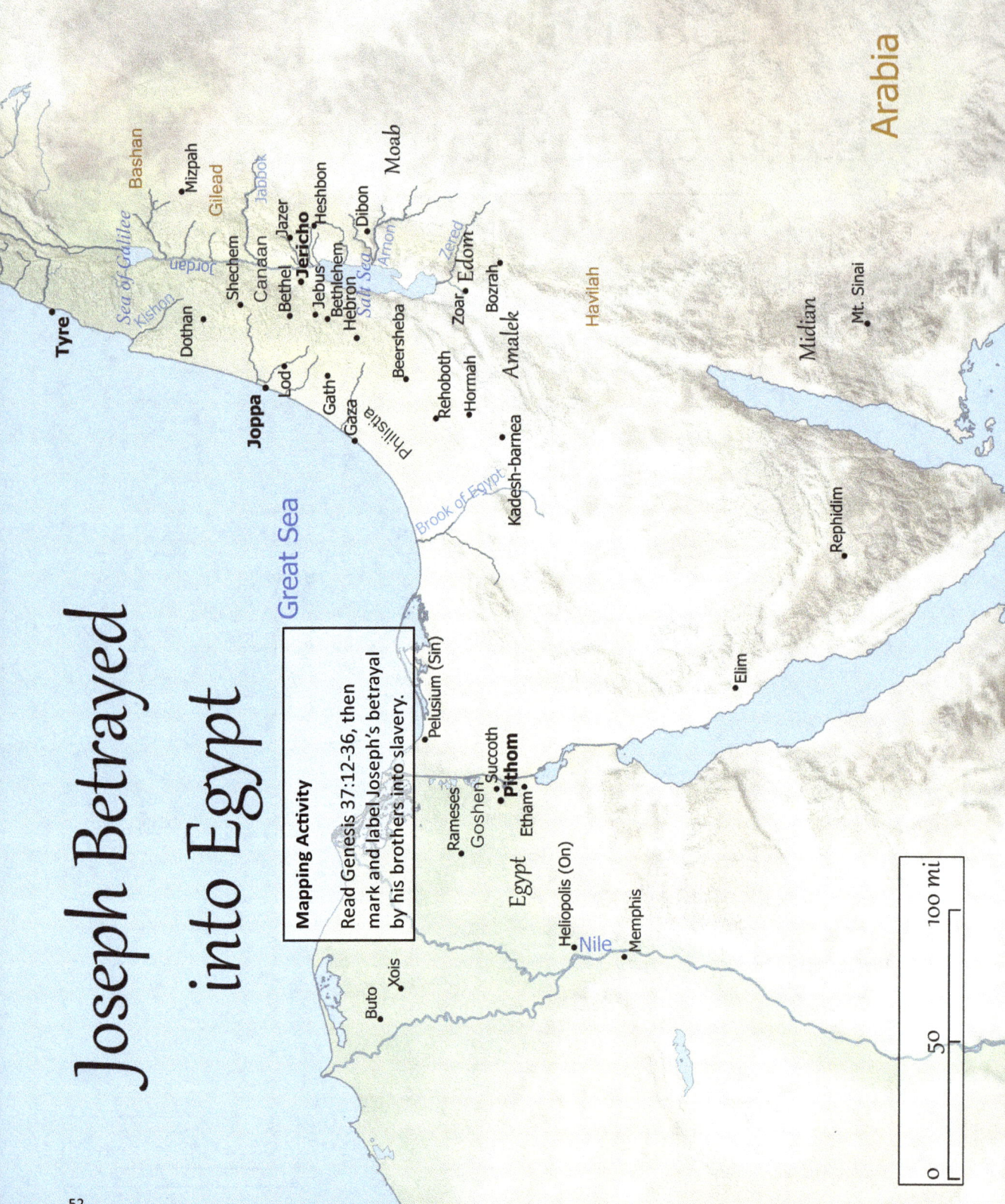

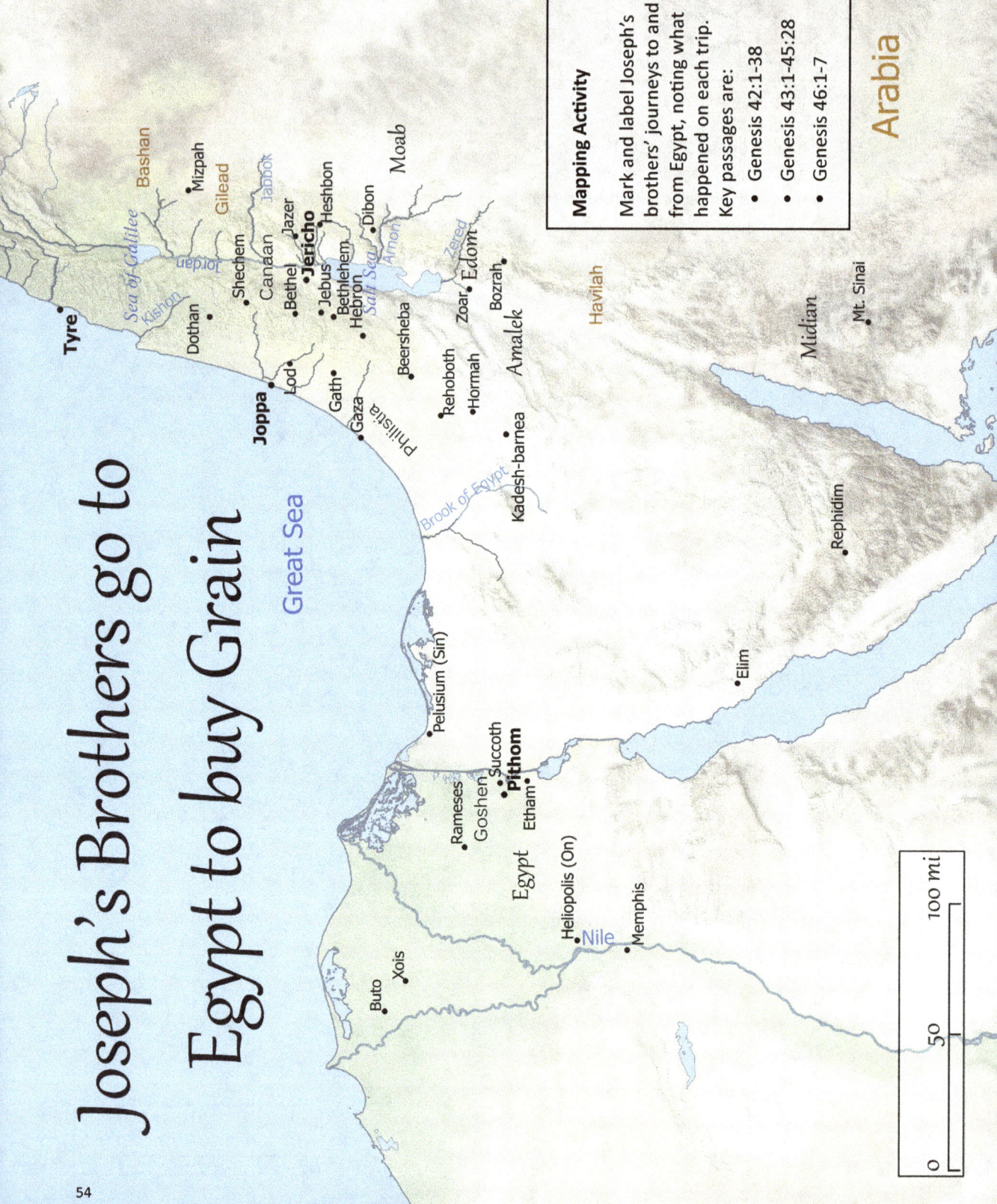

The Exodus From Egypt

Nuweiba Beach Crossing -- Sinai at Jabal al-Lawz

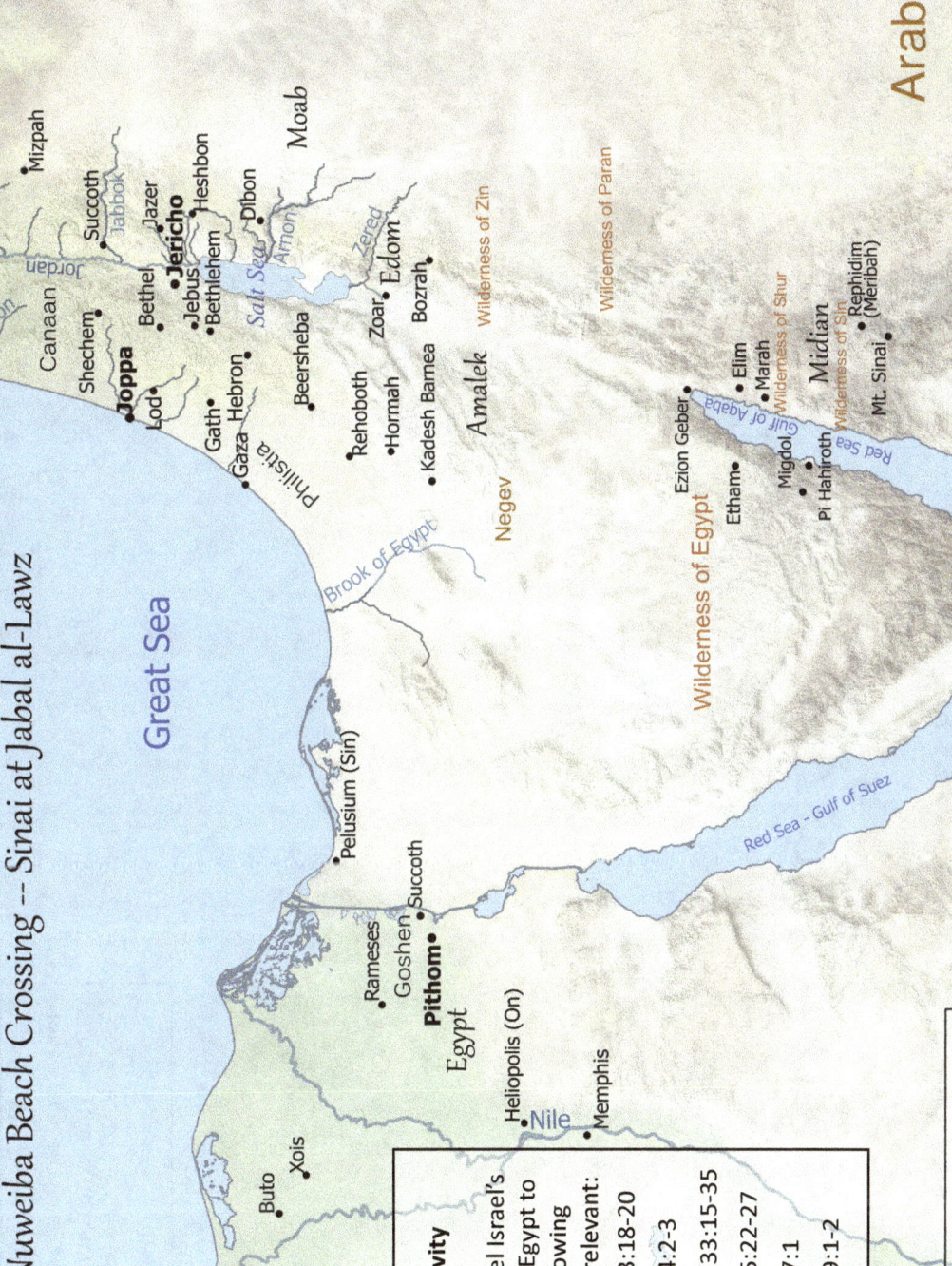

Mapping Activity

Mark and label Israel's journey from Egypt to Sinai. The following passages are relevant:

- Exodus 13:18-20
- Exodus 14:2-3
- Numbers 33:15-35
- Exodus 15:22-27
- Exodus 17:1
- Exodus 19:1-2

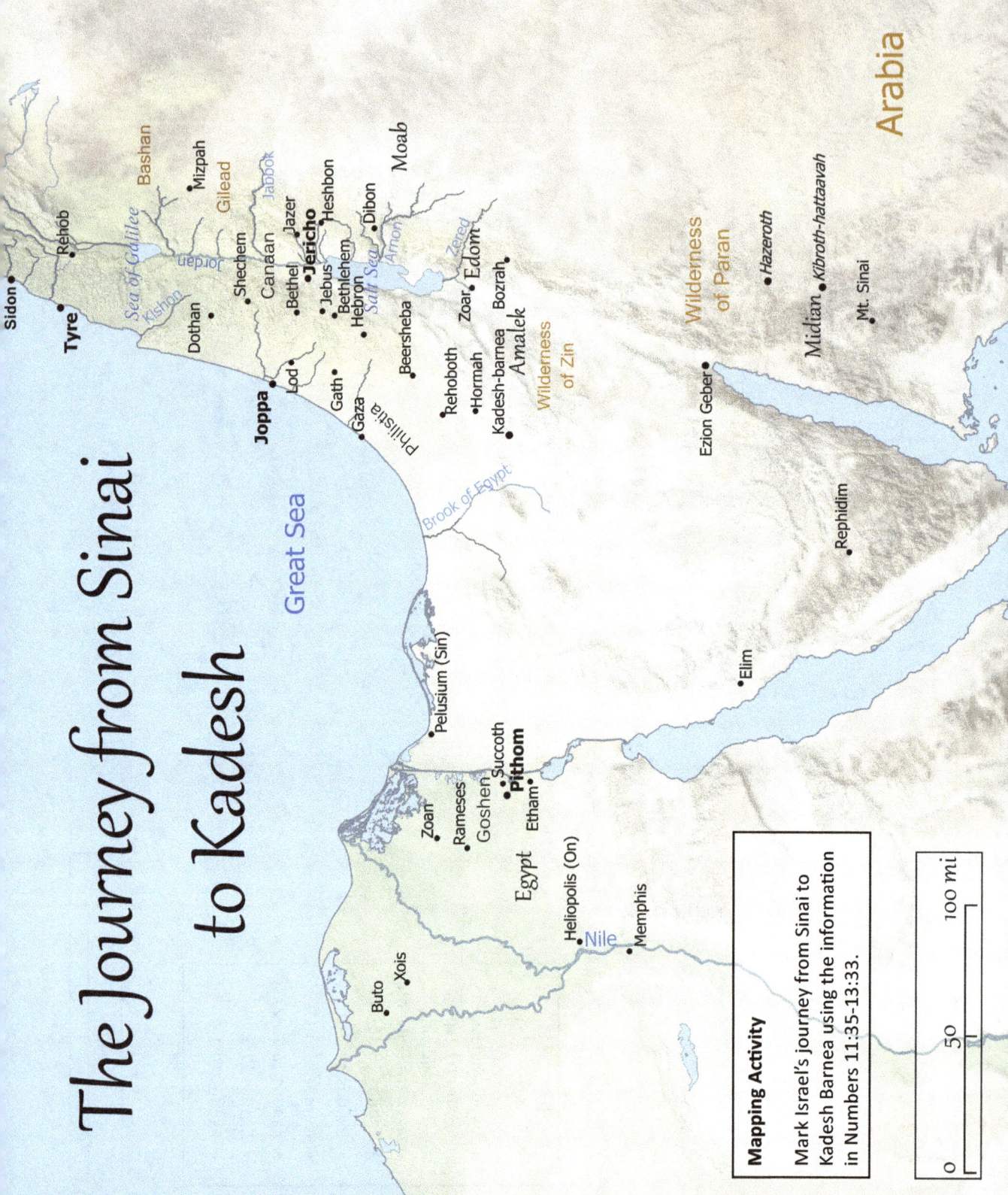

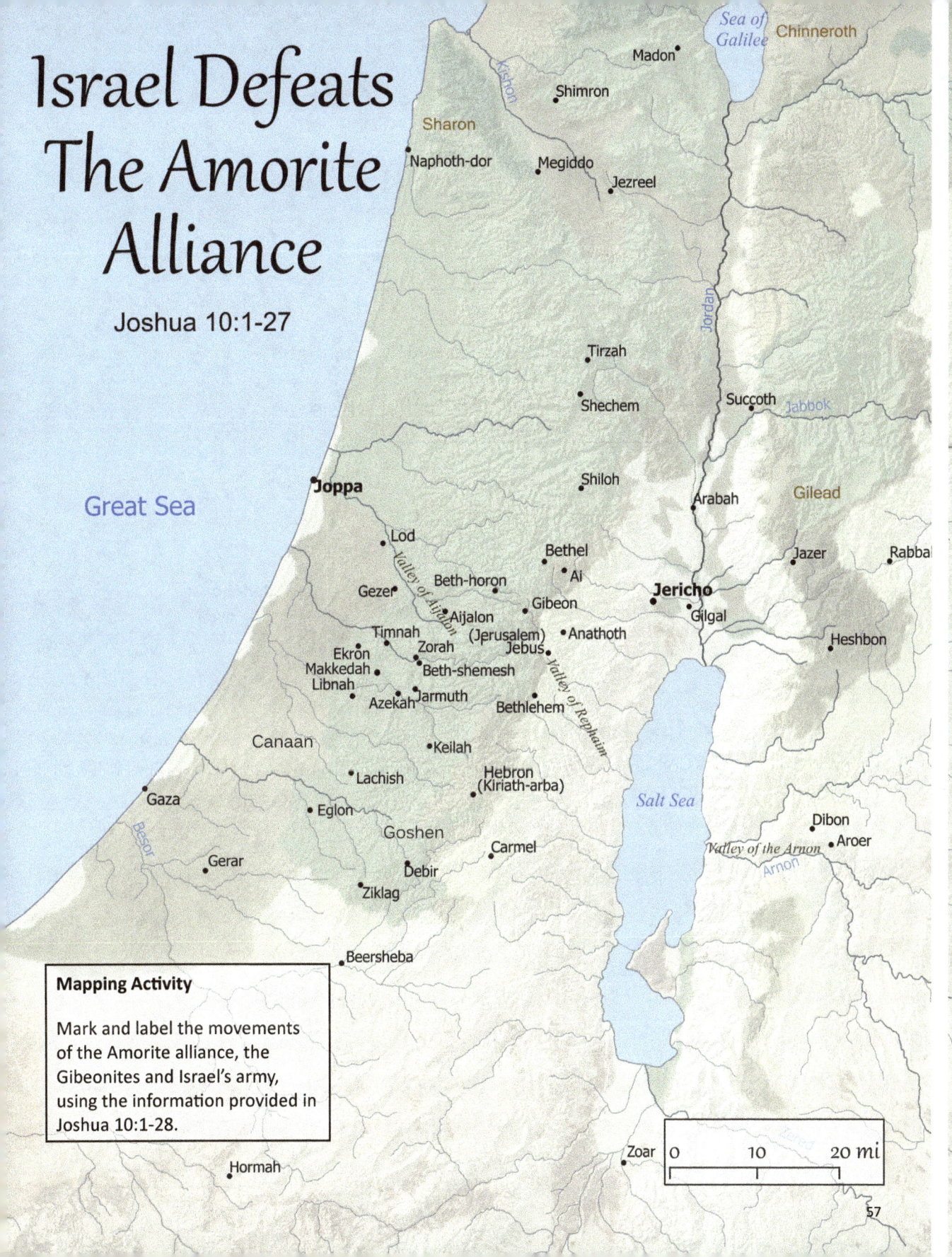

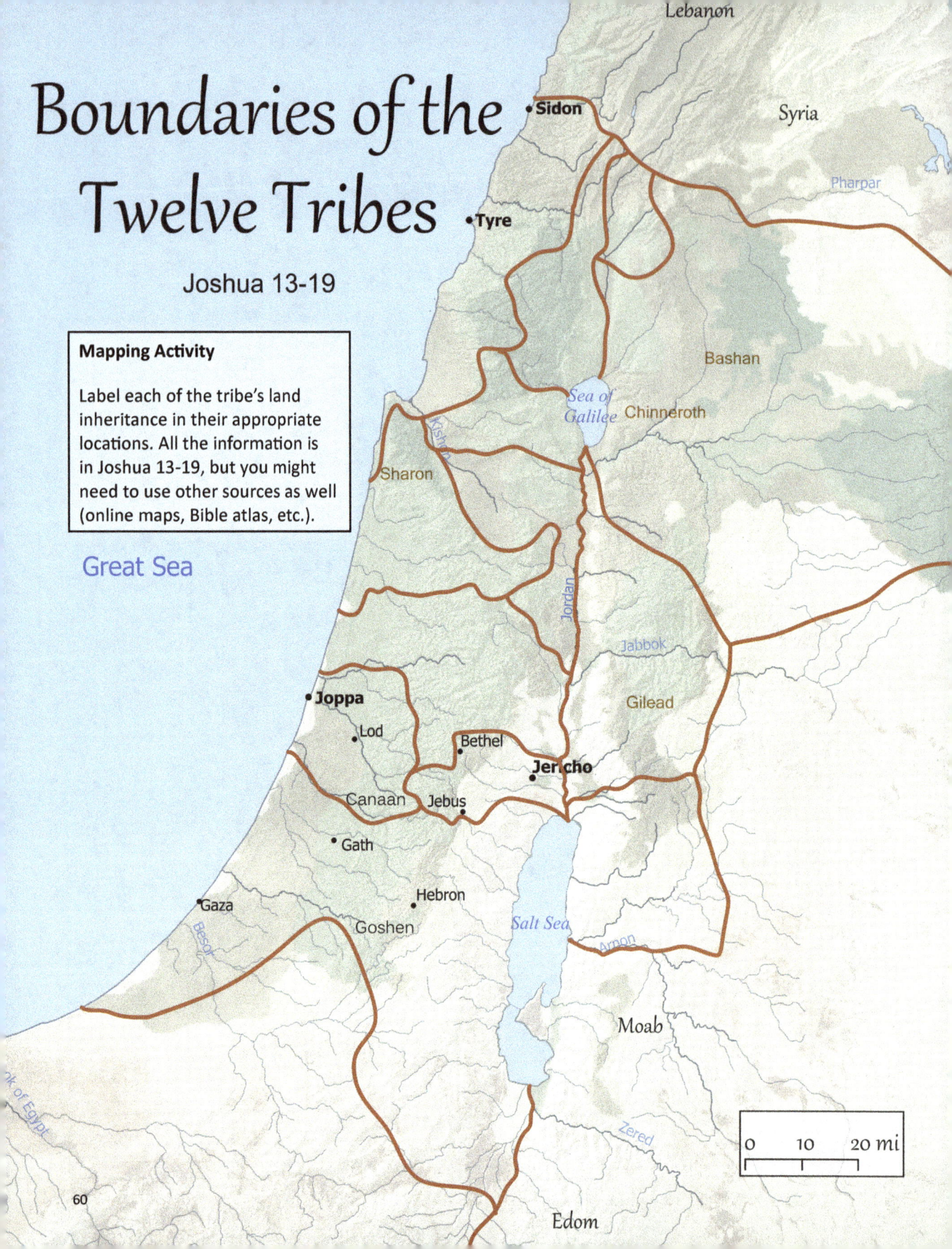

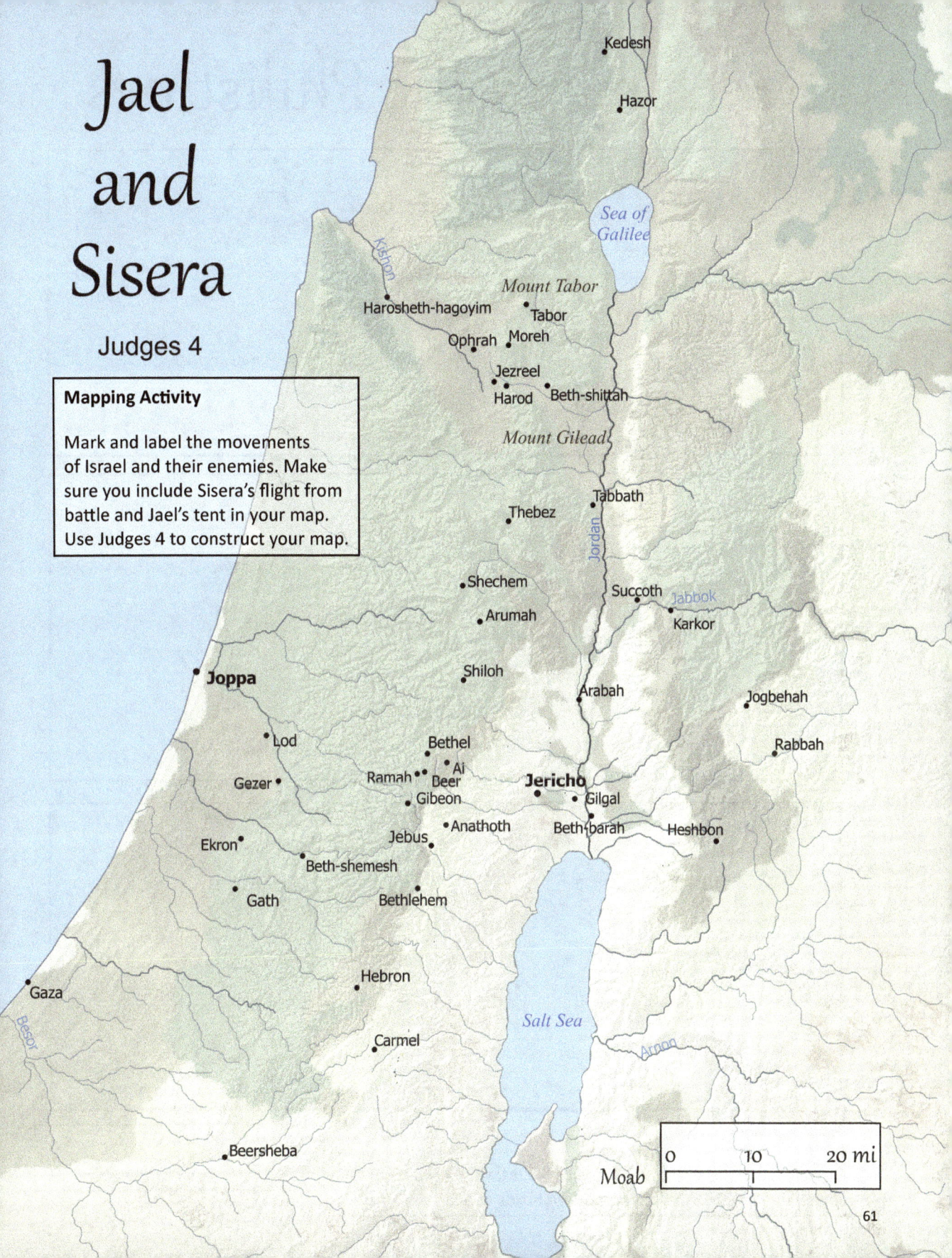

Samson and the Philistines

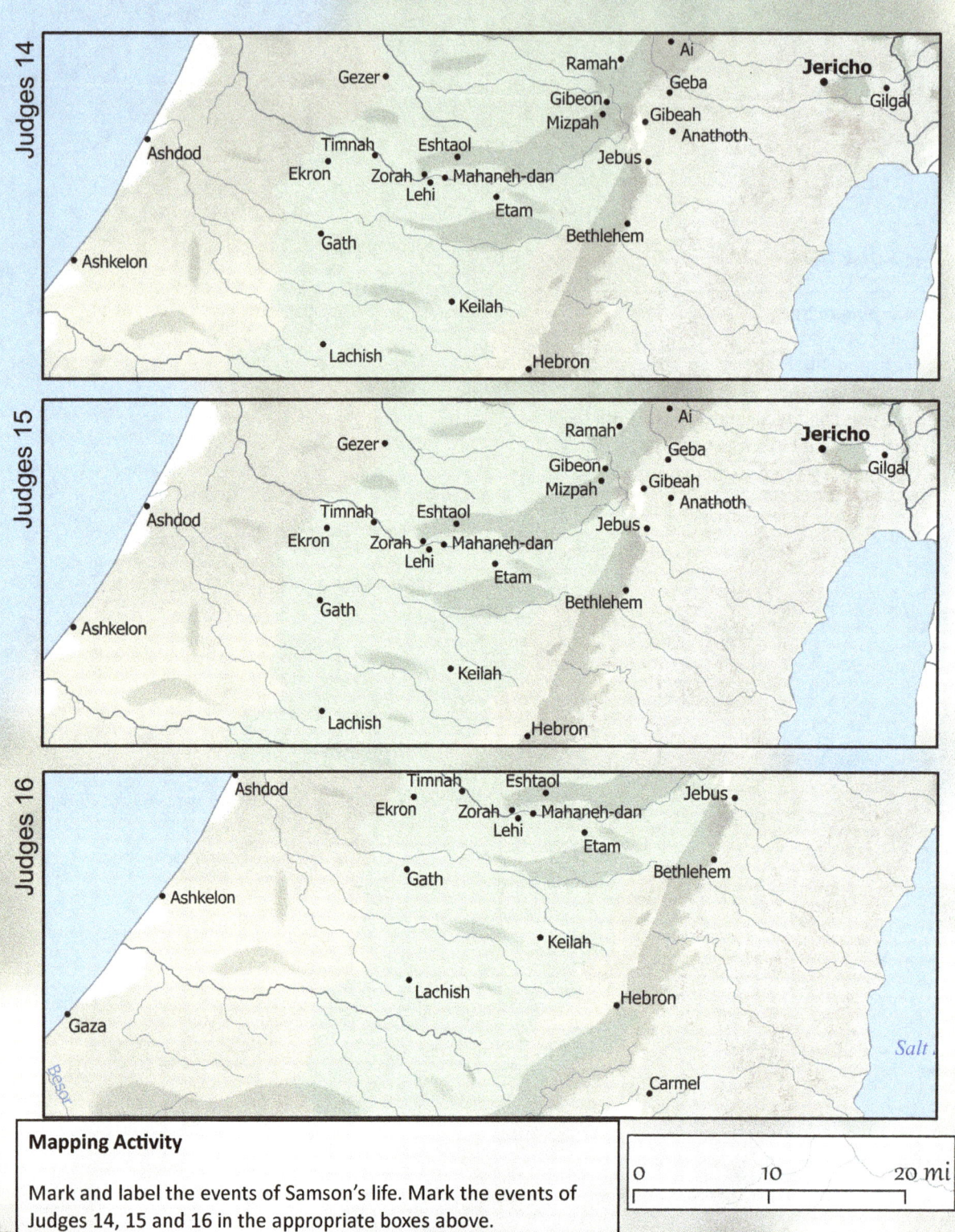

Mapping Activity

Mark and label the events of Samson's life. Mark the events of Judges 14, 15 and 16 in the appropriate boxes above.

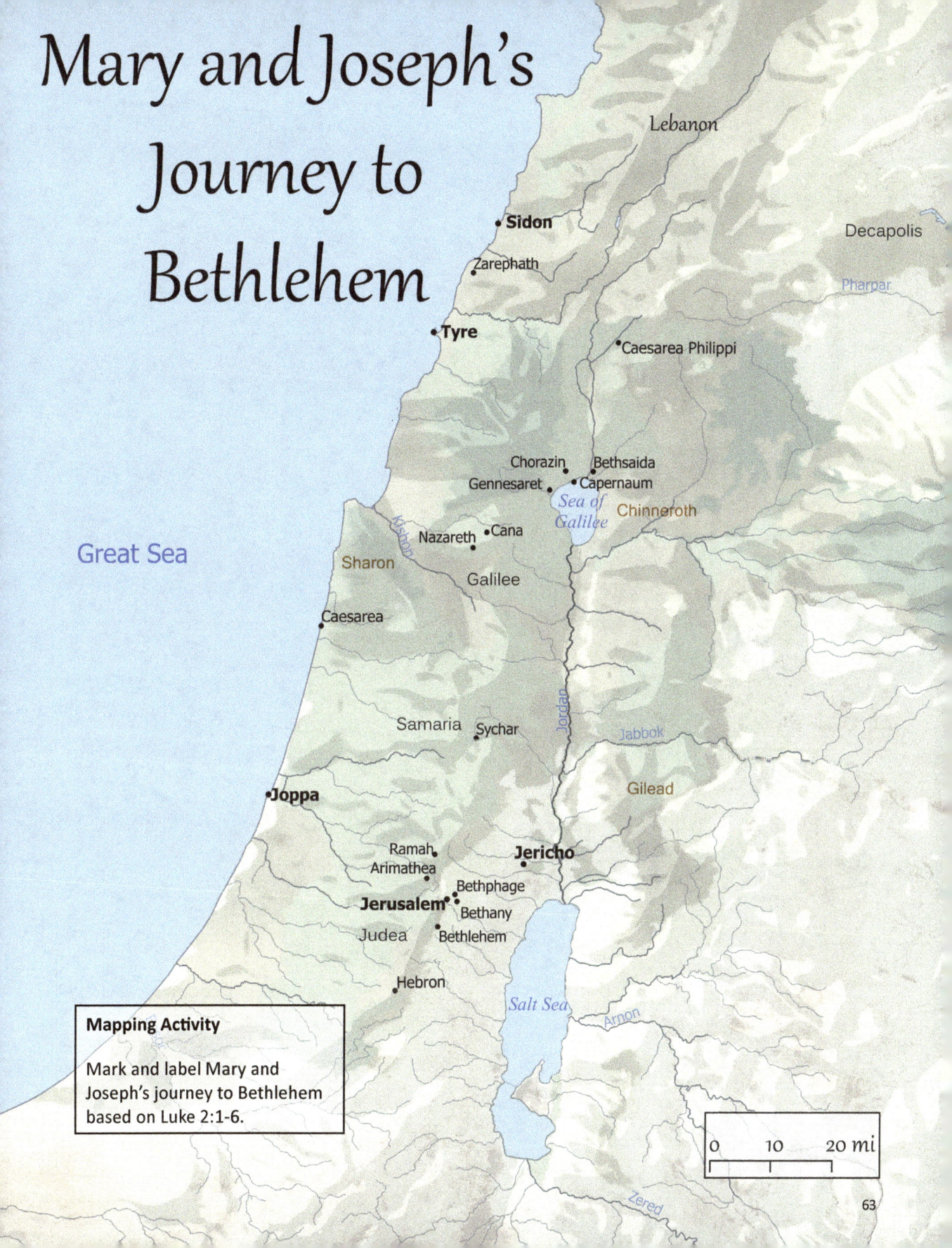

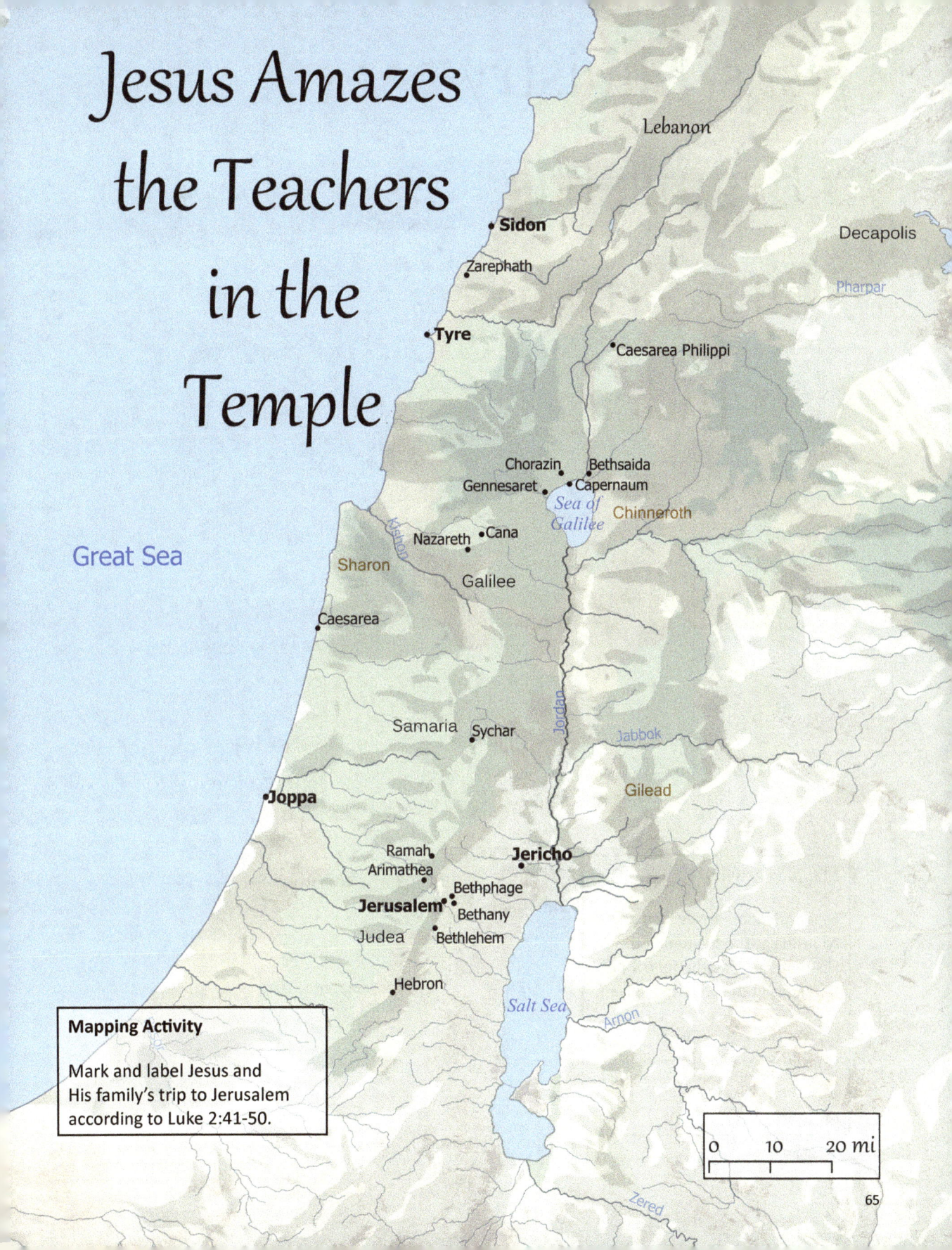

Jesus Amazes the Teachers in the Temple

Mapping Activity

Mark and label Jesus and His family's trip to Jerusalem according to Luke 2:41-50.

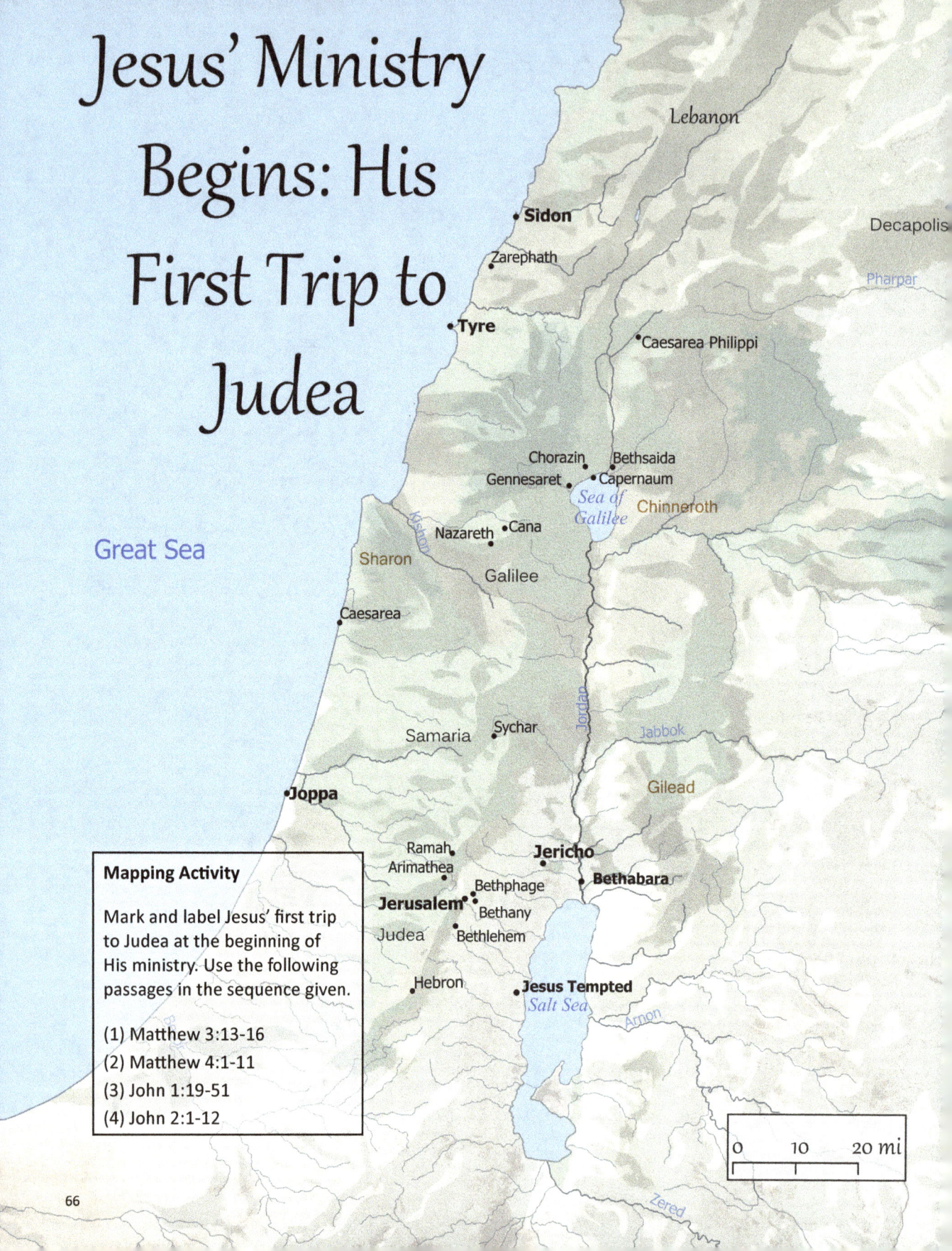

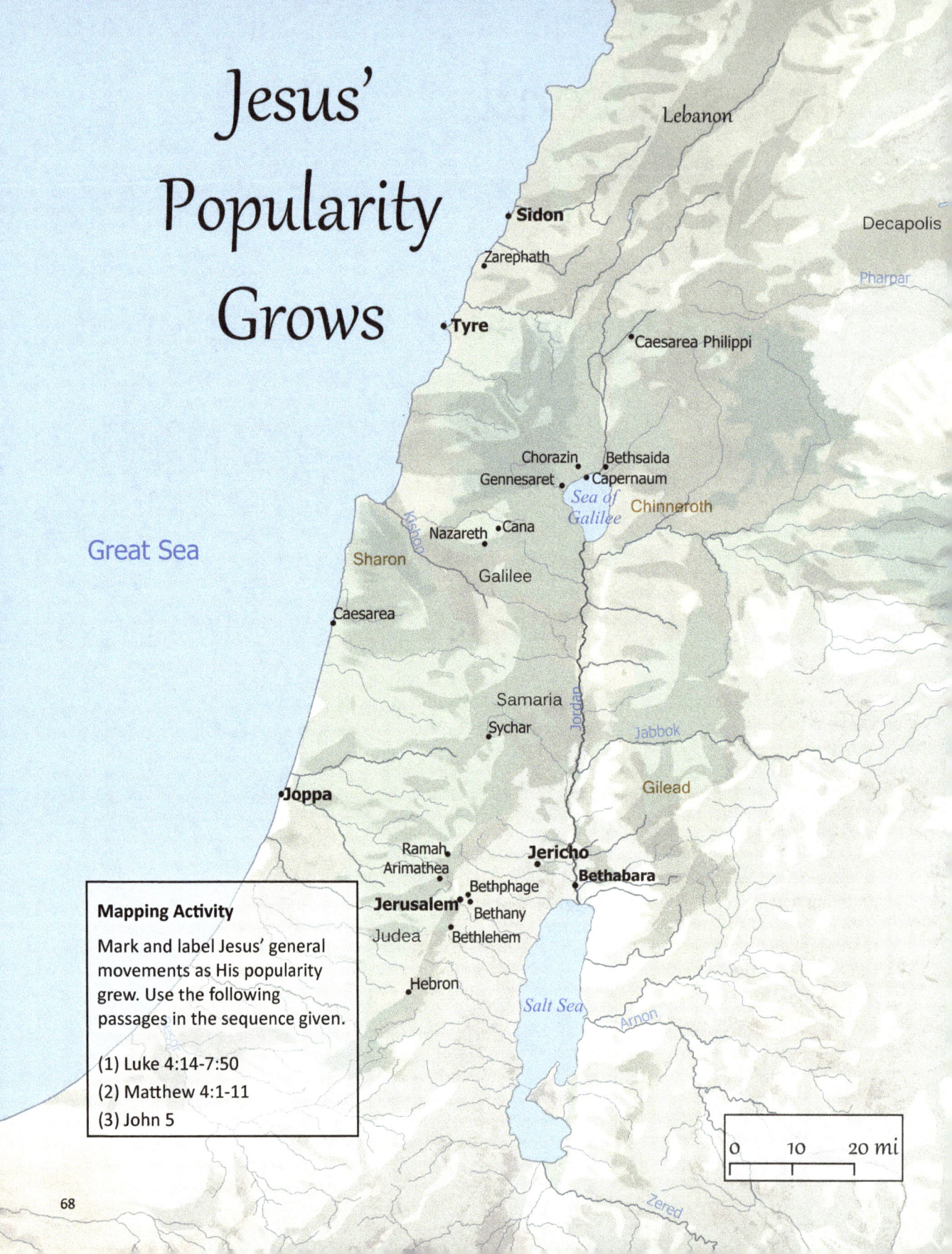

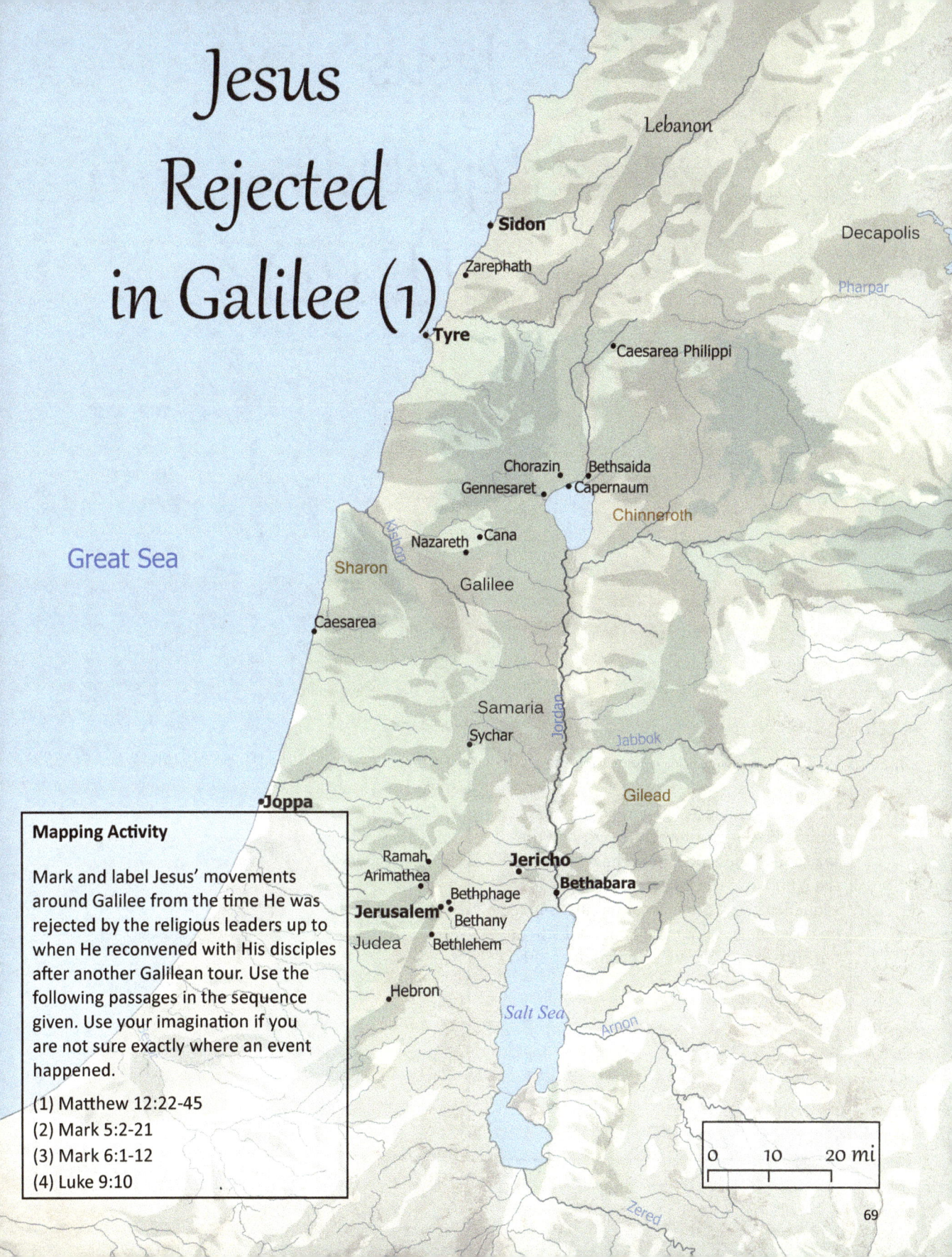

Jesus Rejected in Galilee (2)

Tyre — Jesus delivered the Syrophoenician woman's daughter.

Caesarea Philippi

Chorazin

Bethsaida — Jesus went up on a mountain to pray by Himself.

Capernaum

Gennesaret

Feeding of 5,000

Magdala

Tiberias

Sea of Galilee

Chinneroth

Feeding of 4,000

Mapping Activity

Mark and label Jesus' general movements around Galilee from when He crossed the sea to feed the 5,000 up to the feeding of the 4,000. Use the following passages in the sequence given. Some locations are marked on the map; use your imagination if you are not sure exactly where an event happened.

(1) Luke 9:10
(2) Matt 14:13
(3) Matt 14:22-33
(4) John 6:22-71
(5) Matt 14:34-46
(6) Mark 7:31-8:13

0   5   10 mi

Jesus Rejected in Galilee (3)

Tyre

Caesarea Philippi

Jesus' ministry in the region of Caesarea Philippi

Transfiguration

Chorazin • • Bethsaida
Capernaum •
Gennesaret •
Magdala •
Tiberias •

Sea of Galilee

Chinneroth

Feeding of 4,000

Mapping Activity

Mark and label Jesus' general movements around Galilee from the feeding of the 4,000 up to His return to Galilee after the transfiguration. Use the following passages in the sequence given. Some locations are marked on the map, use your imagination if you are not sure exactly where an event happened.

(1) Mark 7:31-8:13
(2) Matt 15:38
(3) Matt 16:1-12
(4) Matt 16:13, Mark 8:22
(5) Matt 17:1-12

0   5   10 mi

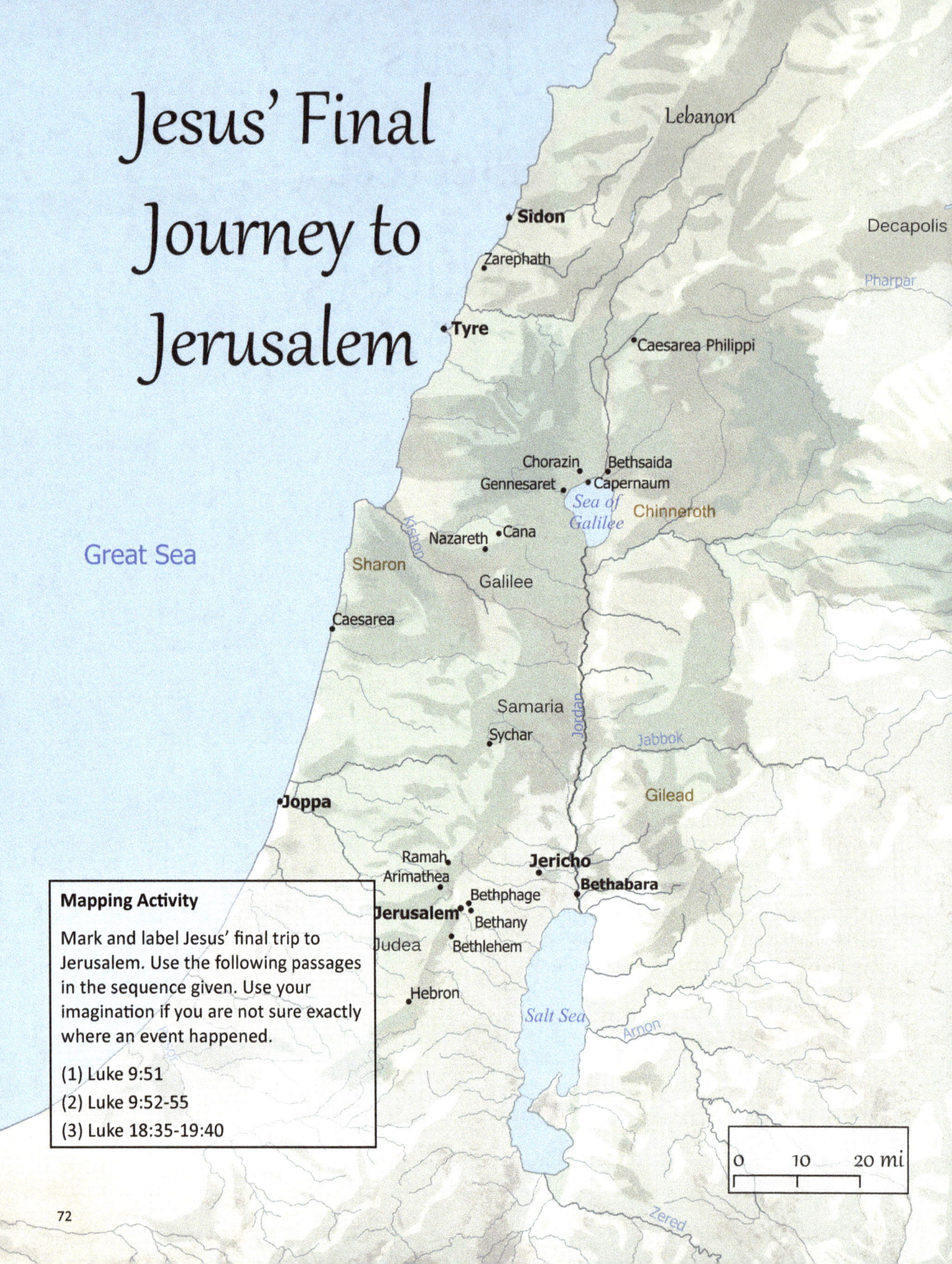

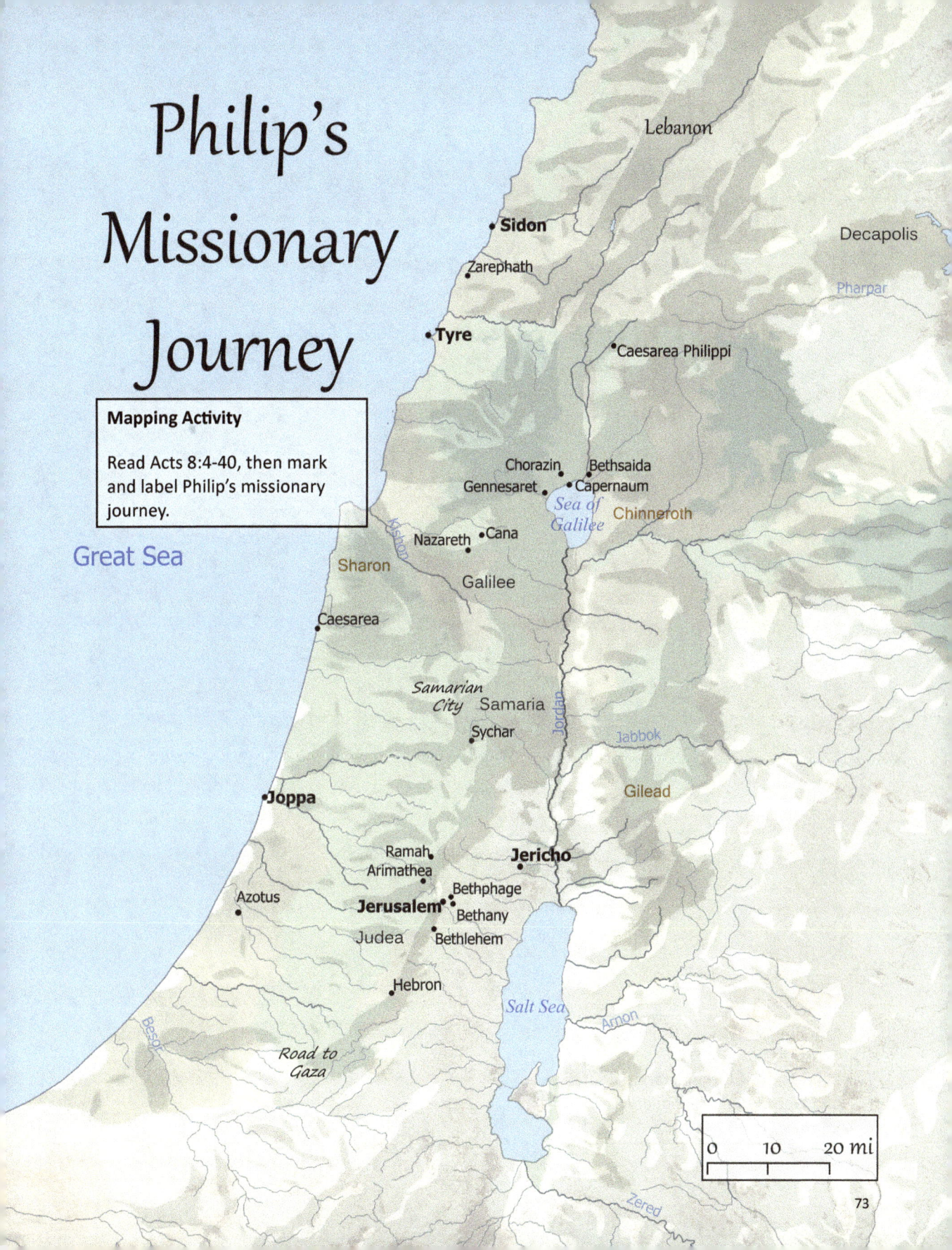

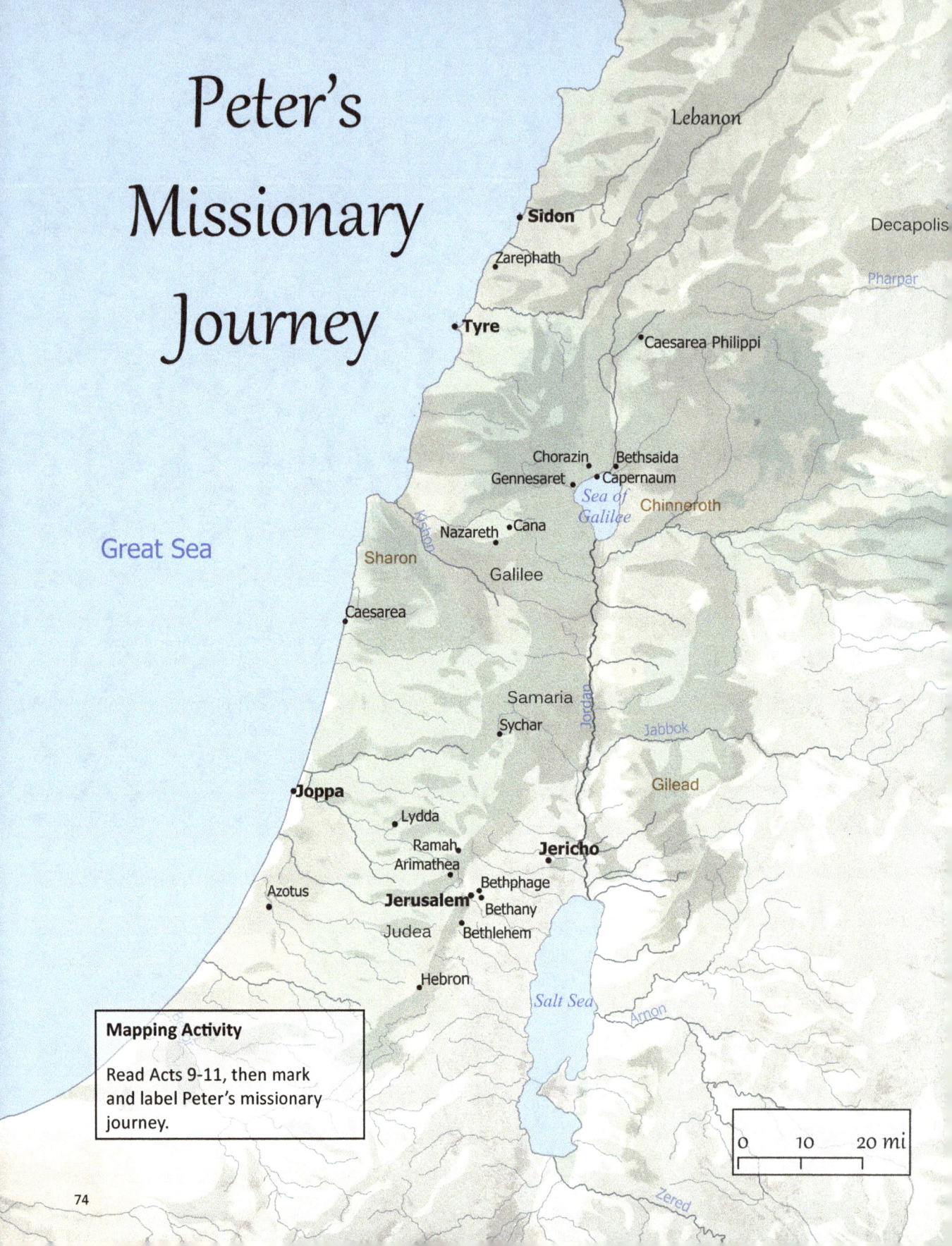

www.ingramcontent.com/pod-product-compliance
Lightning Source LLC
Chambersburg PA
CBHW081339080526
44588CB00017B/2676